DATE DUE	
APR 1 1 2005	
MAY 3 1 2005	

Casino Magazine's Play Smart and Win
(Simon & Schuster/Fireside, 1994)

Casino Games Made Easy (Premier, 1999)

Powerful Profits from Blackjack (Kensington, 2003)

Powerful Profits from Slots (Kensington, 2003)

*Casino GambleTalk: The Language of Gambling and
New Casino Games* (Kensington, 2003)

Powerful Profits from Craps (Kensington, 2003)

Powerful Profits from Video Poker (Kensington, 2003)

Powerful Profits: Winning Strategies for Casino Games
(Kensington, 2004)

Powerful Profits from Keno (Kensington, 2004)

Powerful Profits from Internet Gambling
(Kensington, 2005)

Powerful Profits from Video Slots
(Kensington, 2005)

Powerful Profits from

Casino Table Games

VICTOR H. ROYER

LYLE STUART
Kensington Publishing Corp.
www.kensingtonbooks.com

First printing: September, 2004

10 9 8 7 6 5 4 3 2 1

Printed in the United States of America

ISBN 0-8184-0643-7

This book is gratefully dedicated
to my dear mother,
Georgina S. Royer,
on the occasion of her birthday,
February 28, 2003

"Veni, Vidi, Vici"—I came, I saw, I conquered.

—Julius Caesar

Remember this each time you go to a casino.

"Infinity is the simultaneous occurrence of everything."

—An Australian philosopher

Contents

Foreword

This is the ninth book in my *Powerful Profits* series about casino games, and tenth overall among my current gambling books. I have written about every major casino game you will find in any modern casino and analyzed the games and the strategies that are used to beat them. I've also explained how these older strategies may not necessarily work in today's casinos, and I also presented my own strategies— strategies that I have developed to help in my own gaming, and that will be helpful to those who could learn to play them well. In all these books my point is to show the theory and the methods used to play the theory, and also to show how the real world requires *more* than just theory if you wish to win. Additionally, I show that each of these casino games can be played simply, and that although some of these games may look complicated, in their simplest form they are not. Conversely, I also show that games that appear to be simple—such as slots—are in reality very complex machines and games, and that to win on them you need more than just a coin and a handle to pull, or button to push. Casino games are fun to play, but playing them merely for fun can get expensive. In all my books I show not only how these games can be played for fun, but also for profit. To achieve this, the required knowledge includes knowledge of the game, expertise in the game theory, skills in playing the game, knowledge of the applied theory, ability to adapt to the circumstances, the required bankroll, and, above all, the required personal discipline.

Nothing in life, or in casino gambling, is as simple as it seems, or as complicated as it seems. It all depends on you—the player, the person who does the gaming. The games themselves are there for everybody—the skilled as well as the unskilled. Unfortunately, more than 80 percent of all casino players fall into the category of either the foolish, the misguided, the ignorant, the skill-deficient, or the just plain stupid. In all of nature, everything is divided between the skilled and the unskilled, between the knowledgeable and the ignorant, and between those who know how, and those who don't, and the casinos are a microcosm of all of the various levels of humanity. Some players don't have any clue, and never will. Others are intelligent but don't know that information is available, or don't know how to find it, or don't know which part of the mass of information that is available will be useful to them. Then there are those who simply don't care; they just want to have fun in the casino regardless of how much they lose. That is also okay. Each to his or her own, and everyone is welcome in the casino. Some people are just lucky, and they win in spite of not knowing anything, or not much. And then there are the rest of us—we who aren't so lucky, don't wish to wallow in ignorance, are not reckless, and absolutely *do* want to know how to play better so that our casino visits will cost us less, while we win more and more often. We are these people, the average, ordinary, smart casino players who can do wonders with just the right amount of simple knowledge and the correct and efficient application of some skill. All my books are for these people—for us, you and me. We are the ones.

I have written about each of the major casino games. In this book, I have chosen a slightly different approach. This book discusses many new games, many that are popular but few in number, and some that are not as popular as they once were but are still good games, fun to play, and games that can provide powerful profits. What all these games have in common is that they don't qualify for a book of their own. There just isn't that much to say about them. They are usually either very good or very bad, and their playing strategies need to take that into account. They are also games that often have a "bad reputation," having been in the past classified firmly as "house games," those with such a high house edge that most experts tell players to avoid them. Yet these games persist on the casino floor. Among these games with a "bad rap" is roulette. Although the American roulette holds a steady 5.26 percent edge for the house, this doesn't necessarily mean that it is really a bad game. After all, there are many slots in many casinos that hold 6 percent, 8 percent, or more, yet tens of millions of people play them anyway. Roulette has been so popular in years past that it was overanalyzed into near oblivion. In today's casinos, roulette is usually only tolerated; it is not particularly prized as a "house" game or a player's game. Its aura of mystique is traditionally derived from the European casinos, and from movies such as the James Bond series. But the truth is that even this game can be played profitably—*if you know how.*

Other games are equally misunderstood. Baccarat is one such game, as is Mini-Baccarat. What is usually called the "Big Game Baccarat" is that "posh" game played for high stakes in all those roped-off lounges. Most people therefore think it isn't a game for ordinary folks so they stay away from it. They also avoid Mini-Baccarat, even though that is almost the same game, but played far more simply, and in the main casino pit. Baccarat is among the best house-banked games in any casino. The player bet holds only about 1.2 percent, while the banker bet only about 1.1 percent. The small vig (commission) of 5 percent on banker hands is often reduced in many games. This game is actually better than many video poker games, yet thousands of people avoid baccarat because it looks confusing and intimidating. It is actually a simple game to play, one where most of the time the decision is only an "either-or" situation.

Such misunderstandings plague other games as well. Let It Ride has become a very popular game, but most people don't understand that some bets in the game can often hold almost 20 percent or more for the house, and certainly so when they are combined. Does that make it a really "bad" game? Well, yes and no. There are ways to play this game that can be not just fun, but also profitable. The same goes for Caribbean Stud, which is mostly played as Progressive Caribbean Stud in major casinos, and should never be played unless it *is* a progressive. Other table games such as Double Down Stud, Pai Gow Poker, Three Card Poker, and Super Nines can be found among the table games section of any casino—that area generally known as "the pit." Of course, live poker is becoming even more popular, particularly with the huge success of the major tournaments such as the World Series of Poker at the Horseshoe in Las Vegas, or the nationally televised World Poker Tour.

Then why are all those many poker books so complicated? Can't the casual player find out how to play these games without being bombarded with odds and percentages, holds and discards, and all that headache stuff?

Well, you can. That's what you'll find in this book—*simple explanations of seemingly complex games.* You will also find simple explanations of other games, as well as how to play them immediately without feeling intimidated or confused, and how to play them well. These games are mostly popular among a small core of players who have overcome the games' seeming complexities, odd-looking layouts, or just the intimidation factor of trying something that looks hard. I will show you how easy these games really are, and how to play them without the need for stacks and stacks of cash. In addition, I will show you how you can play comfortably, with enough knowledge to make the games pay as well as they can.

All these casino table games have one thing in common—they are mainstream casino games, but none is sufficiently complex or difficult to require a book all of their own. Therefore, to make these games easily accessible to most people, and to show everyone just how good they can be, I have put them all together in this one book, each with a chapter of its own. None of these chapters is long or demanding. I will simply show you the game, describe how it works and why, and show you how to play it well. Your ability to play these games for powerful profits will therefore be enhanced, because you will find the information that will demystify these games and make it possible for you to enjoy playing them, while at the same time showing you how to play them for value. I have made great efforts to simplify these games so that their stories can be told plainly, and to the point. I didn't want to "waffle on" about this or that aspect of each game, or tell the history of some old strategy. I just want to tell you what the game is, how it works, and how you can play it simply and profitably. And for fun, of course.

In this book, you and I are about to learn enough about the rest of today's casino table games to make us able to play them immediately. With this book as a companion to all of the other books in this series, you will have a complete library of all of the games that are now major staples of twenty-first-century casinos. You'll have the knowledge to acquire the experience, and do so with fun and for profit. That is what I have set out to do with this book, and this series.

Powerful Profits from

Casino Table Games

Baccarat and Mini-Baccarat

Baccarat is a significantly misunderstood game, needlessly avoided by players who think it is only for the rich. Many baccarat lounges offer games with stakes as low as $10 per bet—a far cry from the hundreds of thousands that some high rollers will wager on baccarat. It is because of these high rollers, however, that the average casino player shies away from a game that is actually among the best casino house-banked table games. Even though many casinos have tried to overcome this perception by offering the very same game as a main pit table game, called "Mini-Baccarat" or "Mini-Bac" for short, that entrenched perception remains in the minds of casino players. Perhaps it is because of all those James Bond pictures in which slick James sits at a fancy table in a fancy foreign casino and plays baccarat for millions of dollars per hand. This may happen in casinos in the United States, and the rest of the world, but it isn't the only reality. The real truth is that many thousands more players play the game for $25 and $50 and $100 per hand—small stakes by those standards of the high rollers or movie stars. This is actually the "bread and butter" of the casino. Though many "whales"—very rich gamblers—may lose several million dollars a day, it is actually those smaller players who make it possible for the casinos to continue to offer this game. Baccarat is very labor intensive and can be a slow game. Combine this with the fact that it is among the lowest-hold house games in any casino, and the casinos have to win huge sums just to pay for the operations of the game.

Although losers will mathematically outnumber winners—since any game that holds more than it pays cannot be a positive expectation game for the players—this is nevertheless a game that offers most of the fun, great casino atmosphere, and a good bet to boot. It isn't a game just for the rich or the "pretty people" or the movie stars. It is a game that can be a good bet for anyone who knows how to play it. Just because some players frequenting this game bet huge amounts of money, it doesn't mean they are somehow smarter than you, or play better. Many of these high rollers are actually lousy players, and that is also one of the factors that allows casinos to keep offering this game.

The main problem that regular casino players encounter is the intimidation factor. The game is played in fancy lounges where regular folks think they "don't belong." These same folks think they must bring loads of cash to play there. The seeming complexity of the game also tends to turn them off. All those cards, those moves, that confusing table layout, and the pomposity—well, it's just a tad too much for the burger-and-fries crowd.

Well, I'm part of that burger-and-fries crowd, and I tell you that all those fears are hogwash. While I enjoy getting dressed up when I go to a nice casino, I've played in my jeans and cowboy shirt, and played for $10 and $25 a hand among players who bet from $1,000 to $200,000 a hand, at the same table, and no one gave me grief. I was just another player, enjoying my game. All it takes to overcome any of those fears is to know the game, and what to do. Not being ignorant, or slowing down the game is all anyone asks— players as well as casinos. Know the game, know what to do, then play. No one will bother you or say you are not rich enough to be there. So don't be afraid of baccarat. It is a good casino game, compared with many of the other games offered, and you can play it without fear, intimidation, or anxiety. Here's what you'll need to know to play this game as well as it can be played.

INTRODUCTION TO BACCARAT

As with all table games, you will begin by changing your cash money into gaming chips. In Main Baccarat (often called "Big Game Baccarat"), these gaming chips are larger than regular casino chips. There is absolutely no reason for this other than the aura of special importance that baccarat seeks to cultivate. Perhaps the casinos think that players will feel better about betting large amounts if they have big chips in their hands. But no matter how big these chips are, they function in exactly the same way as any other gaming chips in play throughout the casino. They can be changed for cash if you wish, or for regular casino chips.

At the baccarat table it doesn't matter which seat you take. Unlike blackjack, where position selection can be advantageous in a game with more players—especially if you count cards or are playing one of my observation-based methods—in American baccarat you are not playing against the other players or against the house. Your betting action is solely against the cards. It therefore makes no difference on what the other players bet, or how much, or in what order the cards are dealt. Even if a designated player at the baccarat table does draw the cards, no player decisions are involved. Whether any additional cards are drawn depends entirely on the strict set of rules governing the draw of such extra cards. Consequently, there is no possibility that a player in the position in front of you will receive the cards you would otherwise have received.

Chances are that if you sit down at a baccarat table the game will already be in progress. Very rarely are baccarat tables unoccupied. Many casinos employ house players, called "shills," a couple of whom are often seated at the baccarat table so that potential customers won't have to be the first to sit down or have to play alone. The shills are paid employees of the casino. They play with house money; they don't get to keep any winnings, but they don't lose either. Shills in baccarat are just there to occupy seats. When a sufficient number of customers arrive, the house players leave, returning only if the table becomes empty again. Baccarat shills have no effect on your hands. If, however, you feel uncomfortable about knowing whether or not there are any shills at the table, just ask the casino pit boss to tell you. By law, casinos must identify shills if asked.

Baccarat is played with eight standard decks of cards, no jokers, all shuffled together. When the game is at the point of a new shuffle—either at the very beginning of the game or when the cards dealt have reached the cut card, as in blackjack—one of the dealers will call out "shuffle" and begin to shuffle the cards. When the shuffle is completed, one of the customers will be asked to cut the deck and the cut decks will then be placed in the shoe, ready for dealing. At this point one of the dealers, usually the one who did the shuffle, will turn up the first card out. Whatever the value of this first card is indicates how many cards will be burned. If, for example, this first card out is 6, the dealer will burn six cards (none of which the players see), placing them in the discard tray along with that first card out. The game is now ready to be played.

The shoe containing the eight shuffled decks is called

"the bank," because in many traditional (or European) games the person holding it actually has to back all the bets and therefore really is the banker. This is not the case in American baccarat. In American baccarat the player holding the bank has no specific advantage over other players. That player does not win any more money, does not have to bet on the bank hand, is not responsible for paying winning bets, makes no choices affecting the draw of extra cards, and will not collect any losing bets. This action is merely a cosmetic copy of the European version of baccarat. Unlike European baccarat, where players can play for or buy the bank, in American baccarat the bank is simply given to the player seated immediately to the right of the dealer (position 7) at the beginning of the new game. Each player at the table is then given the bank in turn, and can hold the bank as long as the bank wins. Once it loses, the bank moves to the player on his or her right, counterclockwise.

Before any cards are dealt, all players at the table make their bets and dealing takes place. The player holding the bank deals out four cards—two sets of two cards—with the first and third cards going to the official player's hand, and the second and fourth cards to the banker's hand. The banker's hand cards are tucked under the side of the shoe by the player who holds the bank and is dealing, while the player's hand cards are given by the caller, using that odd paddle, to one of the other players—usually the player who made the biggest bet on the player's hand. This designated player then picks up the first two cards, looks at them, and tosses them face up to the caller, who then arranges them in the center of the table in a special area marked on the table layout as "player." Now the player who holds the bank picks up the two bank hand cards he had tucked under the side of the shoe, looks at the bank hand cards, and also tosses them over to the caller, who arranges them in that same special area in the center of the table marked on the layout as "banker."

This area is directly above (or next to) the one marked "player." Again, remember that these two areas are separate from the betting areas, also so named; they are located in the center of the table layout and used only to differentiate between which cards have been dealt to which hand. To make all this easier to understand, please take a look at Figure 1, the typical layout of a baccarat table.

Although these moves in baccarat make the game seem complicated, I wish to point out one more time that they are really quite unnecessary and have absolutely no effect on the outcome of the game. They are just a relic from European baccarat in which the banker and the player in fact *do* control the cards and decisions for drawing cards and standing. Not so in this American version, whereby the hand's final values would be exactly the same even if none of these moves were made by the players, but were simply dealt by the dealer (which is the case in Mini-Baccarat, a low-limit version of the game usually dealt on a blackjack-sized table in the main casino).

Players can make bets at the conclusion of any hand, or after a new shuffle. There are only three betting areas available, each clearly marked and displayed on the table layout in front of each player position. These are bets on the "bank" hand, on the "player" hand, or on the "tied" hand. To make any one such bet, you place your gaming chips in the area so marked. You can make one, two, or all three bets at the same time, but to bet all three is automatically to lose at least one hand, and more often than not two hands—not a good idea.

Value of Hands and Rules

The object of this game is to place a wager on the hand that will, at the close of dealing, be closest to "9" in total value,

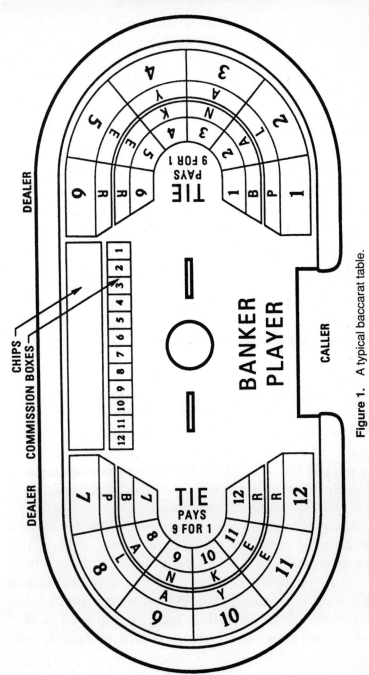

Figure 1. A typical baccarat table.

without going over "9." This is somewhat similar to black-jack, where the object of the game is often colloquially under-stood as reaching the value "21," or as close to it, without going over. Unlike in blackjack, however, the value of the cards in baccarat is calculated differently. To understand how the cards in baccarat are counted, all you have to remember is that all "10-value" cards and face cards are counted as "0"—zero. Aces are counted as "1," and all other cards count for their face value. The various suits—hearts, dia-monds, clubs, and spades—don't matter and play no role in winning/losing decisions. Therefore, for example, when the bank hand has a king and a "2" as the first two cards dealt, the value of this bank hand is "2." The king would count as "10" in blackjack, but in baccarat counts as "0." So, when you add 0 + 2 you end up with 2. Depending on the added value of the first two cards drawn for the bank hand and the player hand, other cards may be drawn as well. The rules for drawing a third card follow.

Rules for the Drawing of Cards in Baccarat

When the player hand has a two-card total from 0 to 5, the player hand must draw a third card. If the player hand has a two-card combination of 6 or 7, the player hand must stand, and if either that player hand or the bank hand has a total of 8 or 9, called a "natural," both must stand.

The rules for bank hands are a little different and de-pend on what cards the player hand draws. If the player hand draws 0, 1, or 2, the bank hand must draw a third card. If the player hand draws 3, 4, 5, or 6, the bank hand will draw a third card depending on which third card is drawn by the player hand. If the bank hand draws 7, 8, or 9, the bank hand must stand, regardless of what the player hand draws.

The best two hands in baccarat are a two-card total of 8 or 9. These are the "natural" hands, and no further cards are drawn. If either the player hand or the bank hand draws such a natural on the first two cards out, the hand is over and the winner is whichever hand drew the highest natural. If, for example, the bank hand draws a two-card total of 9, and the player hand a two-card total of 8, both are naturals, both hands stand, but the bank hand wins 9 over 8.

There are additional details on when the bank hand draws additional cards, or the player hand draws further cards, but these will not help you understand the game (I will show you a chart a little later). In all games of American baccarat, the dealers call for the draw of the cards or draw the cards, so you don't have to be concerned with intimate details of the game. The information supplied here will explain how and why decisions are made, but the ultimate outcome depends *only* on the cards. How you bet will determine if you win and how much you win. For those of you who may be interested in a more detailed explanation of when baccarat hands are hit, or when they stand, here's how it works:

If either the player or the banker has a total of an 8 or a 9, they both stand. This rule overrides all other rules. If the player's total is 5 or less, the player hits; otherwise the player stands. If the player stands, then the banker hits on a total of 5 or less. If the player does hit then the chart on page 10 shows if the banker hits (H) or stands (S). Here's how to read this chart: *If* the banker's total is that shown, *and* the player's hand *draws a third card, then* the banker's hand does as the chart shows. For example: if the banker's hand total is 6, and the player's hand draws a third card that is a 7, then the banker's hand must draw another card—hit. Don't be concerned if this looks confusing. In all instances of baccarat play in major U.S. casinos, the dealers call for the action, including Mini-Bac games in the main pit. The chart simply shows how these decisions are reached, and why.

Drawing or Standing in Baccarat

BANKER'S SCORE					PLAYER'S THIRD CARD					
	0	1	2	3	4	5	6	7	8	9
7	S	S	S	S	S	S	S	S	S	S
6	S	S	S	S	S	S	H	H	S	S
5	S	S	S	S	H	H	H	H	S	S
4	S	S	H	H	H	H	H	H	S	S
3	H	H	H	H	H	H	H	H	S	H
2	H	H	H	H	H	H	H	H	H	H
1	H	H	H	H	H	H	H	H	H	H
0	H	H	H	H	H	H	H	H	H	H

The score of the player and dealer are compared; the winner is the one that is greater. Winning bets on the banker pay 19-to-20 (or even money less a 5 percent commission); winning bets on the player pay 1-to-1; winning bets on a tie usually pay 8-to-1 (often shown as 9-*for*-1).

How to Bet

There are three betting options in modern American baccarat, as played in major casino resorts.

- Bet on player hand
- Bet on bank hand
- Bet on tied hand

Player hand

To bet on the player hand means you place your gaming chips in the area in front of where you are sitting marked "player." You can bet any amount from the table minimum to the table maximum. When betting on the player hand you are betting that at the end of all drawing and dealing, the cards drawn for the player hand will have a total value greater than the value of the bank hand. For example, if the player hand draws king-2-6, and the bank hand draws 3-jack-ace, the player hand wins. Player hand total is 8, and bank hand total is 4. If the player hand wins, as in this example, all other bets lose. Because you backed the player hand—the winning hand in this case—you will be paid even money and will not be charged any commission.

Bank hand

If you bet on the bank hand, and the above example is reversed, the bank hand would win. If the bank hand wins, all other bets lose. In this case you will be paid even money, but you will be charged the standard 5 percent commission on the winning total. This commission, known as "vigorish," or "vig" for short, will not be immediately deducted from your winnings. Instead, the dealer will place the commission in a commission box that is numbered to correspond to the number of your seat. This indicates that you owe the house that amount. You can settle this commission at any time, but you *must* settle it before leaving the table. Some casinos offer lower commissions on bank hands in Big Game Baccarat in an effort to attract more of the high rollers. Major casinos often advertise 4 percent commission, and on special occasions even 2 percent. For casual baccarat players it will make little difference in the short term, but it can make a big difference to high rollers. In Las Vegas such high rollers usually play baccarat in one of the upper-end casinos, such as Bellagio, Caesars Palace, Mirage, MGM Grand, Las Vegas Hilton, Bally's, Paris, or Mandalay Bay.

It is for players of this caliber that casinos offer the lower vig. And for such players the difference is profound, as simple mathematics will quickly prove. If you bet big—in the hundreds of thousands of dollars per hand as is common for many such high-rolling players—a lower vig will make a big difference to your win expectations. But if all you are after is a game whose favorable odds will offer a good gaming experience, but have no intention of betting your life savings on each hand, do not be overly concerned with vig offers. Even if you consistently bet on the bank hand, and win, the overall amount of commission for the time you spend at the game, and amount of total action you give the casino, will not amount to enough to pass up a baccarat game that offers the standard 5 percent vig in favor of a game offering a 4 percent vig. Also, these lower vig games often have high minimum bet requirements, again putting such games almost out of reach of the casual player.

Tied hand

Betting on tied hand means that you are betting that *both* the player hand and the bank hand *will tie* after all cards are drawn. For example: the player hand draws jack-5-2, for a total of 7, and the bank hand draws ace-3-3, also for a total of 7. With a total of 7, both player and bank have to stand, therefore the hand results in a tie. If this happens, and you bet the tie, your bet will be paid at 8:1, and no vig is charged.

To bet a tie hand, place your wager in the area marked "tie," and into the box with your corresponding seat number. This betting area looks the same as the commission area, but if you make a mistake the dealers will ask what bet you are making and you can tell them. You can also simply toss the money you wish to bet into the center of the table and call out to the dealer that you want this placed on the tied hand. Betting the tie is basically a side bet in baccarat. It sounds like a good bet, but tied hands in baccarat are quite rare because the rules for hitting and standing offer so many options to break up possible ties. With eight decks all shuffled together, the flow of any six cards dealt at random, whose ultimate total value as counted by baccarat rules will be equal, is near impossible. Yes, it happens, and yes, it can happen several times in a row, but this is quite rare.

The House Edge

Except for the tie bet, baccarat is one of the best bets in the casino. The following chart shows the house edge on all available bets. Usually a tie will pay 8:1 but in some casinos it may pay 9:1, either as a means of attracting more players, or as a periodic promotion. If you find this, however, pay close attention to the other details of the game. Often an increase in this payoff also means that the game may have a higher minimum bet requirement, either on the whole table or just on the tie bet. As with all casino gambling, it is always a good idea to learn as much as you can about every game and all the various ways in which it can be altered, and then practice this simple rule: If it looks too good to be true, it usually is. This is sound advice for any casino game that looks easy, and particularly for any casino's offer of an increased payoff for some events. This doesn't mean you shouldn't play there, or that game, or wager on that event. It just means you should take a quick step back, look at other elements of the game, or offer, or event, and compare them with the standard. If all else is equal, then this will be a better game. If not, well, then, at least you know enough to look before you leap.

Probabilities in Eight-Deck Baccarat

BET	COMBINATIONS	PROBABILITY (%)	HOUSE EDGE (%)
Bank	2,292,252,566,437,888	45.86	1.06
Player	2,230,518,282,592,256	44.62	1.24
Tie	475,627,426,473,216	9.52	14.36

If the tie bet pays 9:1 the house edge on that bet drops to 4.80 percent.

Lowered Commission Baccarat

Some casinos offer a 4 percent commission on the banker bet on their big table game. This lowers the house edge on that bet to 0.60 percent. The following chart shows the house edge on the banker bet for a commission of 0 percent to 5 percent.

COMMISSION (%)	HOUSE EDGE (%)
5	1.06
4	0.60
3	0.14
2	-0.32
0	-1.24

The commission—or vig, which as you now know is short for "vigorish"—is charged *only* on the banker hands, and *only* if the banker hand wins. If you bet on the banker hand and lose, all you will lose is your wager and not anything extra, as you would if commission (vig) was charged on all such bets. (If that were the case, no one would ever play baccarat.) Knowing the percentage charged for the vig is important, particularly if you are a high roller. It is still important even if you are a small bettor, making, for example, bets of only $25 per hand, which is traditionally the table minimum in most Big Game Baccarat lounges. If you wager on a banker hand at $25, and win, you will be charged a 5 percent vig in most casinos. This means that your "win" just "cost" you $1.25 (5 percent of $25). This vig is not immediately deducted from your bet, as I have said earlier, largely because to do so would slow down the game. You will be asked to settle all such commission "dues" before you leave the table, so be sure not to run out of money before you go.

The importance of this vig should be obvious, even to

players with small stakes, such as that $25 wager I used as an example. I have often played baccarat for various amounts, but mostly at no more than from $25 to $100 a wager, except the time I bet $10,000 at the Mohegan Sun in Connecticut. That was a great ride. I won, and wound up playing for from $1,500 to $5,000 per hand for quite a while, before leaving to go back to Foxwoods, where I was staying and playing poker at the time. At these amounts, the charge for the vig is very important, but it's also important for any amount you wager, because the higher the vig, the more it will "cost" you to win on the banker hands. As I have pointed out in all my books, the costs of the wagers are just as important as the minimizing of losses and the maximizing of wins. Therefore, if you find a game that offers a lower vig, and there aren't any tricks to the game where the costs are increased somewhere else in some other subtle alteration to the game, then that is the game you should play. By reducing the vig to only 4 percent, which is quite common in many casinos, your cost per win, even at the $25 per bet level, results in a saving of 25 cents each time you win your bet on the banker hand, because at 4 percent vig your commission charge will be only $1, and not the $1.25 that is the case in games with the 5 percent vig. Therefore, for each four hands you win, you will pocket an extra $1, because that won't be swallowed up by the casino's charge for these bets. You can easily see how this can translate into large amounts of money saved over time for the smaller player, and for each hand for players who bet big.

A baccarat player who bets $100,000 per hand—and there are many of them in all casinos, especially in Las Vegas—would save $1,000 in commission on a 4 percent vig game for *each* banker hand bet won. This significantly contributes to the player's favorable odds, and, conversely, decreases the casino's expected win on such games. That's why casinos don't always offer it, but also why many do—

because they will attract the bigger players and, since baccarat is a negative expectation game for the players, the house will eventually win. Still, baccarat is a good game. With a house edge of only 1.06 percent on the banker hands, and only 1.26 percent on the player hands at the 5 percent traditional vig rate, this is still among the best house-banked casino table games. Therefore, if you can find a casino that offers one of the rare low-vig games, take a careful look at the rest of the game and, if nothing else is altered, dive right in. You're about to play one of the best casino games, and for less cost.

Keeping Score

When you sit down at a baccarat game you will most likely be given a pencil and a chart. This chart has several rows of boxes on it, identified at the top with the words "bank," "player," and "tie." This card is offered because baccarat players like to keep track of trends in hands. It is a good idea to do this. I have often said that short-term trends are the key to winning, and especially so in baccarat. Cards, no matter how they are shuffled, often tend to run in groups. These groupings can translate into winning trends for bank or player hands in baccarat with almost startling frequency. The chart that you are given is a tool offered by the casinos to make tracking such trends easier for players. It is yet one more way in which casinos cater to the big players, but it can also serve the casual player. Each time the player hand wins, check the box under "player." Each time the bank hand wins, do the same under "bank," and similarly for a tied hand. Soon you will see a pattern emerge, and you can use this to assist your betting strategy.

I should point out however that this is no guarantee of winning. It is merely a tool, and the very fact that casinos offer it to players should tell you something about its potential success rate. If this were the end-all tool for winning, it would most likely be banned by the casinos, not freely offered. It can offer a guide to short-term trends, but each hand is a separate event, and cards have no memory. Its only real advantage to the player can be called psychological, but *any* form of assistance in determining likely trends should be used to the full advantage it can provide.

Simple Strategy

If you win a player hand bet in baccarat, you will be paid even money. If you win a bank hand you will be paid even money, but you will lose the 5 percent vig, which you have to pay before leaving the table. If you bet the tie hand and win, you will be paid 8:1, charged no vig, but these hands do not occur often enough to warrant a mention in strategy. As an introduction, the best way to approach baccarat is as follows:

- Keep track of short-term trends by using the chart card provided by the casino. If you are not offered one, ask for it.
- Bet into any short-term trend you see, but be ready to alternate your player hand and bank hand bets. Trends change, and can be as short as two hands, or as long as ten hands in a row (or more). These are averages based on observation and play.
- Bet the table *minimum* when you begin. If you win, play with the money you won. If you win again, press your bet by one chip each time you win. The idea is to play with the house money as much as possible and to bet into winning streaks, not losing ones.
- If you lose a bet, go back to the table minimum.

- If you see trends alternating between player and bank hands, bet accordingly.
- Bet the tie hand occasionally, especially if you see that the flow of cards have been close to a tie, and a tie has not occurred for some time—but bet only the table minimum (unless you are a big winner, in which case bet whatever you think warrants the risk—but remember that it *is* a big risk to bet any tie hand anytime).
- Because bank hands have a slight edge over player hands, bet bank hands twice to any one player hand bet, *unless* you have spotted a trend in favor of player hands.

These simple suggestions offer a basic framework for betting baccarat. They are by no means the end-all of strategy play, but will provide a better, smarter opportunity for the first-time or casual baccarat player. Greater proficiency in baccarat will come from personal experience as you play the game more, and longer. As you do this you will be in a better position to make your own personal choices. The purpose of these suggestions for simple strategy is to provide you with a beginning framework, always mindful of the fact that baccarat is a game of pure chance and that any win expectation is to be based on betting correctly into short-term trends.

Counting Cards in Baccarat

Not many people know that it is possible to count cards in baccarat. While the theory of card counting in baccarat can produce a very exact count that actually helps to turn events into a player's favor, the unfortunate truth is that such a theory is all but impossible to accomplish. There are many reasons for this, but the most telling is the simple fact of the vast complexity of such a card-counting method when applied to a real game in an actual casino. In theory, this works perfectly, because in the laboratory analysis such card-counting systems do work. In baccarat, a series of 100 million hands produces results that, when quantified, create a theoretically workable card-counting strategy whereby the player assigns certain values to each hand, then proceeds to arrive at a "true count" by using the same principles for such determinations as used in similar blackjack card-counting strategies. In baccarat, this produces a workable format that allows the player to make a series of decisions that positively affect the player's results. Unfortunately this theory also suffers from the same problems as the companion card-counting theories for blackjack: although perfectly understandable under laboratory conditions, the system falls apart in the real world.

First, it is so extraordinarily difficult physically and mentally, that not even a quorum of Mensa members would be able to keep track of it. Second, because of the burn cards and discards, deck penetration, and other cards you don't see, even this count automatically starts at a disadvantage because the counter has to simply "guess" at the very beginning at the composition of the deck, and then continue guessing as the other cards he doesn't see are taken out of play, and those cards behind the cut card are never put in play. This is the greatest fallacy of all card-counting systems, and that's why they simply don't work in the real world. They are useful as a guide, and as part of the general ammunition of knowledge and skills that any gambler should bring to the casino for any game, but these card-counting systems are nothing more than a series of slightly better guesses.

There is, however, a big difference between blackjack card-counting systems and those that can theoretically be applied to baccarat. Blackjack card-counting systems are far more useful and are much easier to do and learn. Although most modern casinos no longer allow you to play that way, or do not offer blackjack games whereby you can use such card-counting systems to best effect, there is still the possibility that they can be used. In my book *Powerful Profits from Blackjack,* I show how to learn the simple "PM count," and how to calculate and use the "true count." The true count is one of the principles also used in counting cards in baccarat. Even though these counting systems are hard to do, and now even harder to put into practice in the real-world casinos, they are better than nothing and can yield a small advantage over the house in some instances. My blackjack book also shows how to use other methods of making the game produce profits, and I have expanded on these methods in my book *Powerful Profits: Winning Strategies for Casino Games.* If you are so inclined, you can adapt those methods also to the baccarat systems. This may require you to do some work for yourself, but it may help you, depending on how well you can do it. It is beyond the scope of this book to explain these systems in depth, but I realize that many players have a tremendous interest in these systems and how they can be used in the real casino. For those of you who have such an interest, I would like to refer you to the book *Winning Baccarat Strategies: The First Effective Card Counting Systems for the Casino Game of Baccarat,* written by my friend and fellow gaming author and columnist Henry J. Tamburin, published by Research Services Unlimited in March 1983. There is also an interesting discussion of baccarat card counting in the chapter titled "Can Baccarat Be Beaten?" in the book *The Theory of Blackjack,* written by Peter A. Griffin, and published by Huntington Press, June 1, 1999. On pages 216 to 223, Griffin concludes that even in Atlantic City, with a more liberal shuffle point than Las Vegas, a player betting $1,000 in positive expectation hands can expect to profit 70 cents an hour.

For those readers who are interested in a more simplified quantification of this issue, I offer the following analysis, a combination of my efforts in conjunction with those of Michael Shackleford, "the Wizard of Odds," as derived from information on his website, www.wizardofodds.com.

ANALYSIS OF THE THEORY OF CARD COUNTING FOR BACCARAT

In either blackjack or baccarat a good first step in developing a card-counting strategy is to determine the effect of removing any given card from the game. The following chart shows the number of banker, player, and tie wins resulting from the removing of one card in an eight-deck shoe. The card removed is indicated in the left column.

CARD REMOVED	POINT VALUE		
	BANKER	PLAYER	TIE
0	188	-178	5,129
1	440	-448	1,293
2	522	-543	-2,392
3	649	-672	-2,141
4	1,157	-1,195	-2,924
5	-827	841	-2,644
6	-1,132	1,128	-11,595
7	-827	817	-10,914
8	-502	533	6,543
9	-231	249	4,260

This chart shows the relative effect of removing one card according to the future probability of a banker, player, and tie win. The greater the number, the more beneficial it is to remove that card. For example, when betting on the banker it is best when 4s leave the deck, and when betting on the player it is best when 6s leave the deck. To adapt this information to a card-counting strategy the player should start with three running counts of zero. As each card is seen as it leaves the shoe, the player should add the point values of that card to each running count. For example if the first card to be played is an 8, then the three running counts would be: banker = -502, player = 533, and tie = 6,543. Of course the player does not have to keep a running track of all three counts. In fact the point values for the banker and the player are nearly the opposite of each other. A high running count for the banker would mean a corresponding low count for the player, and vice versa. In order for any given bet to become advantageous the player should divide the running count by the ratio of cards left in the deck to get the true count. A bet hits zero house edge at the following true counts:

Banker:	105,791
Player:	123,508
Tie:	1,435,963

If you were able to play this strategy perfectly you would notice that the true counts seldom passed the point of zero house edge. The following chart shows the ratio of hands played, based on a sample of 100 million, in which the true count passes the breakeven points above. The left column indicates the ratio of cards dealt before the cards are shuffled.

PENETRATION (%)	POSITIVE EXPECTATION		
	BANKER (%)	PLAYER (%)	TIE (%)
90	0.0131	0.0024	0.0002
95	0.1062	0.0381	0.0092
98	0.5876	0.3700	0.2106

The next chart indicates the expected revenue per 100 bets and a $1,000 wager every time a positive expected value occurred. Please remember that this chart assumes the player is able to keep a *perfect* count and the casino is *not* going to object to the player only making a bet once every 475 hands or less.

PENETRATION (%)	POSITIVE EXPECTATION		
	BANKER (%)	PLAYER (%)	TIE (%)
90	$0.01	$0.00	$0.00
95	$0.20	$0.06	$0.15
98	$2.94	$1.77	$11.93

I hope this shows that *for all practical purposes* baccarat is *not* a countable game. Save yourself some aggravation: if you play baccarat don't try any of the mind-numbing card-counting strategies. Perhaps the only variable of interest here would be if you applied the "exclusion principle," that is, exclude from your count any combination of cards that count to zero. This way you would eliminate the vast majority of cards and events and hands, and would have to concentrate only on the cards and hands that actually constitute numerical values. Of course, this would have the effect of entirely eliminating the tie option—for all practical purposes even if you did want to bet this—which under any such card-counting strategy you would not. By further eliminating from your count any numerical values that would constitute three-card ties, you would be left with only the naturally occurring two-card ties, and that would help you to more easily quantify the remaining cards. This would enable you to more accurately drop the deck down to a workable sequence of possibilities. Make sure you bring plenty of aspirin, or whatever it is you use to calm your headache. Meanwhile, let us now mosey on to some of the more pleasant descriptions of the game, and conclude this chapter with a short description of Mini-Baccarat, as offered in most casinos.

MINI-BACCARAT

Although it does not have all the glamor associated with its posh cousin, Mini-Baccarat is well suited to the casual gambler seeking a good game, favorable odds, and a friendly atmosphere. It is the same game as that found in Main Pit Baccarat and offers the same good odds, but without the pomposity and rigmarole.

Mini-Baccarat is played on a blackjack-sized table with seven player spots and a single dealer. It has none of the needless ceremonies surrounding who deals the cards, who holds the bank, and so on. All the rules and betting options, as well as the vig, are exactly the same as those used in Main Game Baccarat. The only differences are in the table layout, how the dealing takes place, where the cards dealt are arranged, and how many players can sit at the table.

At the Mini-Baccarat table, each player spot has two circles, one above the other, in front of his position. The one closest to the player is marked "player" and the one above it is marked "banker." Above this is a semicircular strip about two inches wide running the length of the table marked "tie" at either end, and divided into numbered areas that directly correspond to the players' positions at the table. Directly in front of the dealer is the chip tray where all house gaming chips are kept, and directly in front of this is the commission box grid. Eight decks of cards are used, as in the Main Pit Baccarat game.

The single dealer—dressed in casino uniform, not a tuxedo—does all the shuffling. A player selected by the dealer cuts the cards after each shuffle, the shuffled and cut decks are placed in the shoe, one card is dealt face up and other cards subsequently burned (depending on the value of that first card)—again the same as the main baccarat game—bets are made by the players, and the hand begins. The dealer deals the first and third card to his or her right, and the second and fourth card to the left. Usually there are no designated areas on the table layout for Mini-Baccarat marked as "banker" and "player" into which these cards are dealt, as in the main baccarat game. But this doesn't matter. The hand dealt to the dealer's right is always the player hand, and the other is always the banker hand. In all other respects the game plays the same as its rich cousin in the main pit.

The advantages of Mini-Baccarat for the casual player are the generally low betting requirements—usually starting with a $5 minimum bet and a $500 maximum bet per hand—and the casual atmosphere, in addition to the good odds the game offers. Another advantage is that Mini-Baccarat tables often have very few players, which gives the dealer time to explain any nuances of the game that you may wish to ask about. It is, therefore, a good introduction to baccarat. In most casinos, rules in Mini-Baccarat are also exactly the same as for Big Game Baccarat, and in all other playing respects the game plays the same. And that, dear friends, is the story of baccarat in a nutshell, and all you'll need to know to play the game well, for fun, and for profits.

PROFESSIONAL BACCARAT

Few professional gamblers select baccarat as their game of choice. Most of those who can still make a living from gambling are poker players, notably the ones who play in poker tournaments, often referred to as the "poker tournament trail." There are many such poker tournaments around the United States, as well as in many European countries and elsewhere in the world. The popularity of this form of professional gambling is easily understood—poker is a game in which the casino (the house, or the owner/operator) does not figure. This means that the house is not a participant in the game, but merely facilitates it. The profit to the house from live poker comes from the rake, which is usually somewhere between 5 percent and 10 percent, with a maximum of between $3 and $5 for most small- to middle-limit games, and $10 maximum for higher-limit games. In poker tournaments, the house takes a cut from the entry fees, usually about 1.6 percent of the total prize pool, or it may charge an up-front fee of several dollars, depending on the kind of tournament it is and what the amounts of the buy-ins may be. Therefore, the poker professional knows immediately what the "costs of the game" will be for him. He knows, or can easily calculate, that the "costs" of playing in a poker tournament are the entry fee plus house take, or house charge. And that's it. In live games, called "ring games," the poker professional can easily calculate the hourly "costs" of his game by the amount of the rake, its percentage, and how often the game will yield the maximum house take. This makes the expense of being a professional poker player much more easily calculable than in other games.

There are also professional gamblers who play blackjack. Although the modern game of blackjack is very hard to beat, it is still possible, under certain circumstances, to do so with skilled play (see my book *Powerful Profits from Blackjack* for more details). What makes these kinds of blackjack games and live poker games different from the other casino games is that they can all be beaten by skill, as expressed through the analysis of mathematical percentages. They are positive expectation games, which means that, when played skillfully, these games can actually overcome the in-built house edge (for blackjack) or the house rake or fee (in poker) and turn the game into one whose mathematical payback percentage is now in the favor of the player. The skillful professional gambler can now calculate not only how much she can win, but also how long it will take and how much it will cost. These are the primary reasons why professional gambling is possible, and particularly so on these two games—blackjack and live poker. Some video poker games can also be played professionally, and for profit—games whose mathematical payback odds are set to pay back more than 100 percent. These games do exist, and if played properly will yield a mathematically identifiable positive expectation percentage in the favor of the player (for more details please refer to my book *Powerful Profits from Video Poker*). If we allow for the inclusion of video poker in those formats, we can now count three casino games that can provide a positive margin for the skilled professional gambler: blackjack, poker, and video poker.

As you can see, baccarat is not included among them. Neither is Craps, or roulette, or any of the other games. This is because all of these are what are called "house-banked games," meaning that the player is playing directly against the house and the house has an in-built edge that always assures it a steady win. These are *negative expectation* games, meaning that no matter how skillful you play them, they cannot be beaten—as understood from within the mathematical model of probabilities and payback percentages. As I have shown in this book, and in my books on the other games, these house edge percentages can be very small, even infinitesimal in some instances, such as Craps (see my book *Powerful Profits from Craps* for details). But this still doesn't allow for these games to yield an actual and identifiable player positive expectation—these are all "house games," by that mathematical definition, and therefore no professional gambler can expect to yield a profit from them. Consequently, the best that any player can do is to select those house games whose in-built house withholding percentage can be lowered by skillful play, or whose standard house edge is already as low as the game can get, under the terms and conditions of its play in the traditional casinos.

Among the house games that are the better bet are baccarat, and, of course, also Mini-Baccarat, where the house edge on both the player and banker hands is very low. Therefore, even though you are giving up some kind of an edge to the house, in this game you aren't giving up a huge edge. As a result, you can play baccarat with the reasonable expectation that you will not lose as much as you would if you were playing a game whose house edge is higher. What this means is that you can count fewer "costs" of the game, thereby providing yourself with a higher bankroll retainer percentage: you simply won't lose as much as fast! This will allow you to last longer in the game, and allow both your skills, and your luck, to prevail for you.

While skillful play in blackjack and poker can result in a complete edge swing in the player's favor, this is not possible for baccarat. However, there are skills involved in baccarat, many of which we have already discussed. Among them are the spotting of trends and variable betting. Although I did mention card counting, I have also shown that it is all but impossible to actually do in the real world, so this will not be regarded here as a skill in this game. Variable betting, and the spotting of trends, and perhaps card tracking may be better skills to apply to the game of baccarat with reasonable success. Since the game's house edge cannot be overcome, the only other way for the game to yield a profit for you will be in the combination of skills, your longevity at the game, and your skillful exploitation of the luck factor, perhaps more easily identified as "skillful betting into positive trends." Doing this will help you make more money from baccarat than you would make otherwise. Such principles of professional play can also be applied to other games, including the more traditional house games with a greater house edge, such as roulette, which I discuss in the next chapter.

If you wish to make baccarat a staple of your advanced or semiprofessional gaming, you will need to know the following crucial information:

- The total possible combinations of hands in baccarat, for the player hand, the banker hand, and the totals
- The probability of each total for each of these hands
- The probability of each total after two cards have been dealt to each player hand and banker hand

To help you with this, I have prepared several charts to show you this information in as clear a format as possible. The first (Figure 2) is the complete breakdown of the occurrences of all hands in baccarat. The second (Figure 3) shows the probability of each final combination of hands. The third (Figure 4) shows the probability of each hand total after the two cards have been dealt to the player and banker hands.

Figures 2 and 3 are based on an eight-deck shoe. Figure 4 shows the probabilities for both the six-deck and the eight-deck shoes, just in case you are playing a game where only six decks are used, which can often be the case in Mini-Baccarat. As previously mentioned, I again wish to thank Michael Shackleford, the Wizard of Odds, for his help with the verification of these calculations, as well as his very valuable assistance with these percentages and figures.

The complete breakdown of all hands in baccarat.

Figure 2

Possible combinations of hand totals for banker and player hands in baccarat, based on an 8-deck shoe.

Banker Total	Player Total					
	0	1	2	3	4	5
0	28979901420544	2463919538560	24214066700288	23748210556928	24642962657280	25228523110400
1	24291119898624	20499217668352	20114458411008	19634953029632	20535822327808	21127406358528
2	24211866148864	20469715722240	20006606104576	19563259723776	20465430315008	21055697346560
3	26957461020672	23203622991872	22766694555648	22250510129408	20521555795968	21104461946880
4	46033607532544	40593010774016	38585331400704	38147840425984	36294133463040	34322188435456
5	46171612971008	40755264745472	42895386193920	45111417946112	41782247059456	39684046743808
6	48639204401152	40608057946112	42768049588224	44979215931392	45802040381440	46435736207360
7	54083703291904	46026293614592	45544433684480	45155412082688	45975559438336	46610049437696
8	85076577230848	57774350200832	57197896224768	56875337277440	57616152412160	58332350017536
9	85351454494720	57948328357888	57372732461056	57051058384896	57790127128576	58535141937152
Total	469796508410880	372517055559936	371465655324672	372517215488256	371426030979072	372435601541376

Figure 2 (cont.)

Possible combinations of hand totals for banker and player hands in baccarat, based on an eight-deck shoe.

Banker Total	Player Total				
	6	7	8	9	Total
0	5737238186936	58350707818496	88188576587776	88370543349760	443735067603968
1	48967402696704	49945260759040	60551359631360	60628881760256	346295882541312
2	4887002718032	49787546013696	60325437726720	60401880698880	345157466980352
3	48999874119680	49957422518272	64689446563840	63310197227520	363761246869760
4	51520246087680	49835600281600	64455840866304	67209934278656	466997733545984
5	56928963244032	55257433686016	67326512491552	67443153604608	503359177443584
6	96170001308416	94910008393728	72372438790144	72499777142784	6051845300090752
7	100883873370112	101717538899968	77910445719552	78043684069376	641950993608704
8	77985646493696	79056148815872	54879416675072	55165968408576	639959843756800
9	78221719912448	79298740000896	55279842324480	55146054060032	641996333062144
Total	66592013627636	668117541187584	665982456134400	668220074600448	4998398275503360

Note: This chart was too long for one page, and that's why it is on two pages. You can easily read it by following the numbered headings under "Player Total."

Figure 3.

Probability of each final combination of hand totals for banker and player hands in baccarat, based on an eight-deck shoe.

Banker Total	Player Total										
	0	1	2	3	4	5	6	7	8	9	Total
0	0.005798	0.004929	0.004844	0.004751	0.004930	0.005047	0.011478	0.011674	0.017643	0.017680	0.088775
1	0.004860	0.004101	0.004024	0.003928	0.004108	0.004227	0.009797	0.009992	0.012114	0.01213	0.069281
2	0.004844	0.004095	0.004003	0.003914	0.004094	0.004212	0.009777	0.009961	0.012069	0.012084	0.069054
3	0.005393	0.004642	0.004555	0.004452	0.004106	0.004222	0.009803	0.009995	0.012942	0.012666	0.072776
4	0.009210	0.008121	0.007720	0.007632	0.007261	0.006867	0.010307	0.009970	0.012895	0.013446	0.093429
5	0.009237	0.008154	0.008582	0.009025	0.008359	0.007939	0.011389	0.011055	0.013470	0.013493	0.100704
6	0.009731	0.008124	0.008556	0.008999	0.009163	0.009290	0.019240	0.018988	0.014479	0.014505	0.121076
7	0.010820	0.009208	0.009112	0.009034	0.009198	0.009325	0.020183	0.020350	0.015587	0.015614	0.128431
8	0.017021	0.011559	0.011443	0.011379	0.011527	0.01167	0.015602	0.015816	0.010979	0.011037	0.128033
9	0.017076	0.011593	0.011478	0.011414	0.011562	0.011711	0.015649	0.015865	0.011060	0.011033	0.128440
Total	0.093989	0.074527	0.074317	0.074527	0.074309	0.074511	0.133227	0.133666	0.133239	0.133687	1

Figure 4.

The probability of each total of banker and player hands in baccarat after the first two cards have been dealt to each.

Total	Six Decks (%)	Eight Decks (%)
0	14.72	14.74
1	9.50	9.50
2	9.45	9.45
3	9.50	9.50
4	9.45	9.45
5	9.50	9.50
6	9.45	9.45
7	9.50	9.50
8	9.45	9.45
9	9.50	9.50
Total	100	100

You should note that the differences are only in tiny fractions of each percentage. Also note that tied hands have been discussed earlier, and that's why they do not appear in these figures. The usefulness of these figures is in the exercise of your skills in actual play, by being able to anticipate the possible composition of the hands as they might be dealt, particularly when practicing pattern and trends recognition. Although this will not assure you of a steady win (as I have said, the game of baccarat is a negative expectation house game) nevertheless, as these figures show, there are certain circumstances where this knowledge will prove helpful. Of course, this all depends on just exactly how deeply you wish to get involved in the analysis of the game, or your own game strategy. Even if you never put these figures into practice as you play, the mere fact that you are now aware of them—regardless of whether you can actually fully comprehend them or their applicability to strategy play in the game—will make you more aware of the cards, and the hands, and the possible patterns or trends that they may display. Even if only casually understood or merely read through here, these facts and charts will provide some lingering carry-over to your actual play, whether you are consciously aware of it or not. It's kind of like second nature, which is something that blackjack players understand when they fully master basic strategy or perhaps some forms of card counting. This knowledge will help you when you aren't even aware of it—in the heat of the moment, and the thrill of the game.

Of course now that we have found out what the probabilities are for the final totals for banker hands and player hands with only the first two cards dealt, what about the probabilities after four cards have been dealt? Remember the rules for drawing of cards in baccarat? Look again at the chart just shown—Figure 4. If you look at that chart first, and then at Figure 5, you will be able to tell the relative odds of the probability of one hand drawing cards or not, as based on the totals of the hands with four cards. This shows you the probability of the banker wins and the player wins as well. Furthermore, here we also show the probability of a tie win, based on the first four cards being dealt. Again, a very interesting exercise in additional knowledge, and one that can have significant impact on your win expectations in baccarat, as well as on your ability to spot and potentially exploit streaks and trends. See Figures 5, 6, and 7.

Figure 5.

Probability of a win for banker hands in baccarat, based on an eight-deck shoe.

Banker total	Player total							
	0	1	2	3	4	5	6	7
0	0.427793	0.40973	0.391882	0.374037	0.356195	0.33765	0.231516	0.15434
1	0.495459	0.426929	0.409234	0.391336	0.373435	0.354619	0.230281	0.153216
2	0.513308	0.496004	0.42693	0.409025	0.391346	0.37253	0.23028	0.153224
3	0.525182	0.513697	0.501957	0.438649	0.4267	0.354636	0.230271	0.154128
4	0.578664	0.60282	0.627004	0.591578	0.326054	0.289715	0.230277	0.153211
5	0.638716	0.674654	0.650906	0.62815	0.604411	0.348888	0.231193	0.154125
6	0.721859	0.710369	0.698539	0.687609	0.675001	0.662331	0	0
7	0.769393	0.769718	0.769708	0.768806	0.769725	0.76881	1	0

Figure 6.

Probability of a win for player hands in baccarat, based on an eight-deck shoe.

Banker total	Player total							
	0	1	2	3	4	5	6	7
0	0.427793	0.495459	0.513308	0.531152	0.548995	0.567741	0.692221	0.769393
1	0.40973	0.426929	0.496004	0.513697	0.531594	0.550413	0.69265	0.769718
2	0.391882	0.409234	0.42693	0.496004	0.513892	0.532501	0.692656	0.769708
3	0.385978	0.397289	0.409025	0.420977	0.484285	0.497143	0.693563	0.768806
4	0.368064	0.343812	0.319906	0.295919	0.331354	0.597782	0.69265	0.769725
5	0.31995	0.283814	0.248357	0.271183	0.294994	0.320049	0.691742	0.76881
6	0.24875	0.200798	0.212631	0.224459	0.236161	0.24891	0	1
7	0.15434	0.153216	0.153224	0.154128	0.153211	0.154125	0	0

Figure 7.

Probability of a tie win for hands in baccarat, based on an eight-deck shoe.

Banker total	Player total							
	0	1	2	3	4	5	6	7
0	0.144414	0.094811	0.094811	0.094811	0.094811	0.094608	0.076263	0.076268
1	0.094811	0.146141	0.094762	0.094968	0.094971	0.094967	0.077068	0.077066
2	0.094811	0.094762	0.146139	0.09497	0.094762	0.094968	0.077064	0.077068
3	0.08884	0.089015	0.089018	0.140375	0.089015	0.148221	0.076166	0.077066
4	0.053272	0.053368	0.05309	0.112503	0.342591	0.112503	0.077073	0.077065
5	0.041335	0.041531	0.100738	0.100667	0.100595	0.331064	0.077065	0.077066
6	0.029391	0.088833	0.08883	0.087932	0.088838	0.088759	1	0
7	0.076268	0.077066	0.077068	0.077066	0.077065	0.077066	0	1

Now firmly empowered with this additional information and detail, you can play the game of baccarat among the very elite of successful baccarat players.

Roulette

Roulette is an extremely simple game. A wheel with numbered pockets mounted inside the sunken dish is spun. Then the croupier (dealer) places a small white ball into a groove around the rim of the dish and spins it in the opposite direction to the spin of the wheel. Gravity eventually causes the ball to fall onto the spinning wheel, where it bounces around until it comes to rest in one of the numbered pockets. Winning and losing depend on where the ball lands and which bets players make prior to the spin. Each spin of the wheel is a new game. All bets are paid before the next spin, and all new bets must be made before the next spin. However, players can often continue to make bets right up to just before the white ball drops down and starts bouncing around the spinning wheel, which the croupier will indicate by calling out "no more bets." Roulette is also one of several casino games, such as traditional reel slots and lounge keno, whereby players are mere spectators and can make no decisions to affect the outcome of the game.

INTRODUCTION TO ROULETTE

When you approach a roulette table, the first thing you do is change your money into roulette gaming chips. Unlike gaming chips used in all other table games, roulette gaming chips show no denominational value. In all the other table games, if you buy a $5 chip you will get a red chip with "$5" printed on it. When you buy roulette chips, the value of each chip is determined either by the value you specify each such chip to have, or automatically by the value corresponding to that table's minimum betting requirement. For example, if the table minimum is 50 cent chips, and you change $20 and do not specify the value of the roulette chips, the croupier will automatically give you forty gaming chips, each of which has a value of 50 cents. However, you can specify the value of these chips over and above table minimum requirements. If instead of a 50 cent value you wanted each chip to have a value of $1, all you have to do is ask the dealer for "twenty dollars in one-dollar chips, please." By doing this you are increasing the value of the roulette chips from the table's minimum. You can specify that the chips you buy have any value from the table minimum up to $5 each. If you specify $5 value chips, then you will get the red chips with the $5 value printed on them. These are the same chips you will normally get in all the other table games. If you intend to bet $25 chips, or $100 chips, then the same applies. The reason for this system is that most roulette players will only bet $1 chips, or chips of lesser values. Of course, this does not prevent you from stacking the chips up. Even if you bought $20 in 50 cent chips, and decided to bet them all on the one number, it would be perfectly okay to do so. In that case you would just stack them all up one on top of the other, on the number you want to bet. If you do this the dealer may suggest that you simply bet four red $5 chips instead, but it makes no difference to the game. No one will bother you or question any of your decisions. All the casino requires is that you make at least the minimum bet, and from that point on if you want to bet a sky-high stack of chips it's fine by them.

Most roulette tables in Nevada and New Jersey casinos will be at the $1 minimum value. Several casinos will also offer the 50 cent version, and a few even a 25 cent minimum. You must remember that winning amounts are calculated based on a $1 bet. So, if the value of your chips is 50 cents, any win you get will be half, in total value, of the amount you would have won if you bet the $1 standard. For 25 cent chips it will be one-fourth of that value.

Since roulette chips don't have their value printed on them, the dealer tells them apart by colors. If there are three players at the table, in addition to you, and all buy in for $20 worth of $1 chips, the dealer wouldn't be able to tell them apart if they were all one color. One-dollar chips used in the other table games in the casino are all the same color, usually cream, or off-white. If all the four players at this roulette table had them, how could the dealer, or the players themselves for that matter, tell who won? In this example, you can receive your chips in blue, the second player in yellow, the third in brown, and the fourth player in green. This tells you apart. The colors themselves do not matter. If you win, your colored chip will designate you as the winner, and you will be paid with chips of the same color. As long as you play at this same table, the color designated to you will be yours.

Bets in roulette can be made in a variety of ways, and are generally divided into two groups: "inside" and "outside." Inside bets are those made inside the numbered grid on the layout, and outside bets are those made outside this grid. For example, a bet on the number "10" will be an inside bet, while a bet on "red" will be an outside bet. The basic differences between inside and outside bets lie in how much you can bet and how much you can win. Table limits for inside bets are, generally, $1 minimum and $100 maximum straight up on any single number, and up to $2,500 in overall spread, while limits on the outside bets are generally $5 minimum and $5,000 or more maximum. Inside bets pay more, but are harder to win. Outside bets pay less, but win more frequently.

Roulette provides the house with a steady 5.26 percent edge over the player. This edge is constant on all bets at every spin of the wheel. It can be so constant because each new spin of the roulette wheel is a new and independent event. Neither the wheel nor the ball remembers any past events, and therefore roulette is among the very few games that allows for such steady house wins. This house edge is derived from the use of the 0 and 00 house numbers, and the fact that the house pays off at less-than-true odds. Since there are thirty-eight total numbers that can become the winning number—with thirty-six on the main layout upon which players can bet plus the two house numbers, on which the players can also bet—but the casino only pays off at 35:1 maximum for the win on any straight-up single number wager, it is pretty clear how this comes about. This is different for European roulette, which only employs the single 0; in this game the house edge is only 2.7 percent overall.

Unlike other table games, players at roulette have no opportunity to reduce this house advantage, such as taking full odds in Craps or playing basic strategy and counting cards in blackjack. But although this information is quite important to the game aficionado, for casual play it makes little difference. Nevertheless, it is important that you know what you're giving up when approaching roulette and to realize the odds against you; this, however, shouldn't deter you from playing roulette since there are indeed some bets that can be very profitable in the short term.

The Layout

The layout indicates the betting possibilities and it is on this layout that players make their bets. It is rectangular in shape. The main portion of this is an area in the center on which are the numbers 1 through 36. These numbers are three deep in rows and alternate in color between red and black. Facing the table from the player's side, looking into the pit, to the left of the layout (referred to as the "top") are the two house numbers: "0" (single zero) and "00" (double zero). These numbers are in green. This makes a total of thirty-eight available numbers, any of which players can bet on either singly or in groups. Closest to the player on the layout are other optional side bets:

- The numbers 1 through 18, meaning players can bet on the first eighteen numbers
- Odd/even, meaning players can bet on odd or even numbers coming up
- Black or red, allowing bets on either color no matter what the number
- The numbers 19 through 36, allowing bets on any of the second eighteen numbers
- First 12, second 12, third 12, known as "dozens," meaning players can make a single bet on any of those twelve numbers showing up
- First row of 12, second row of 12, or the third row of 12, known as "columns," which are the same in total numbers (twelve) as the first, second, and third 12 on the side layout, but instead of playing twelve numbers in a *group*, you are playing twelve numbers in a *row*

Figure 8 shows the traditional American roulette table layout.

43

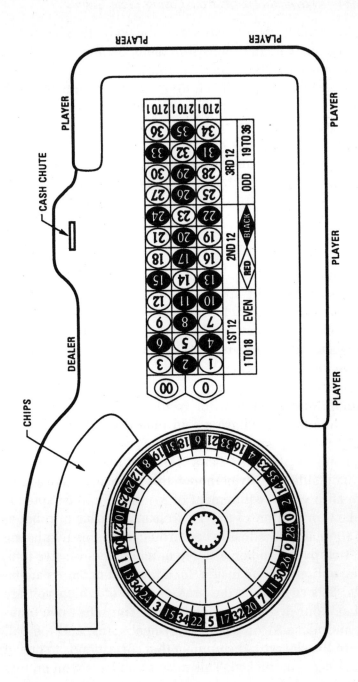

Figure 8. The complete layout for American roulette as it appears in the casino.

This roulette table layout and the roulette wheel have the same thirty-eight numbers on them, painted in the same colors, but *not* in the *same sequence.* This is important to remember because if you bet, for example, 10 and 11, these numbers are next to each other on the table layout, but on diametrically opposite sides on the wheel itself. This was initially designed to prevent people from betting sequential sections, but many modern casinos now offer sequential bets as part of their revitalization efforts for roulette.

How to Bet

The simplest bet is to put your money on a single number, known as a "straight up" bet, also known as "inside bet." This means you place whatever amount you want to bet on one number, and one number only. You have thirty-eight numbers to select: 1 through 36, plus the zero (0) and double zero (00). Be careful which roulette table you select. All roulette tables have a small sign that outlines the betting minimum and maximum for inside and outside bets, but some roulette tables have a sign that also states the minimum "spread" required. This means that this particular table requires players to bet a certain amount on either inside or outside bets. Even though this table may have a minimum chip value requirement of $1, the required "spread" may be a minimum of $5. This means you have to bet at least $5 total on the inside bets. You can do this by placing five $1 chips stacked on a single number, or cover five total betting options on the inside, for a total bet of $5. As an example, let's say this is the kind of table at which you are playing. Your first bet is a total of $5. You select five numbers, and place $1 on each. The wheel spins, and the ball lands in the slot with the number that corresponds to one of the numbers you picked. This means you have won on that number and lost the other four bets. A single number inside bet will pay 35-to-1 (35:1). So, for the $1 bet, you will now get $35 back, plus the $1 stays on the number that won. You can remove that $1, making your total gross take for that spin $36. You can also let that $1 ride for the next spin, but, remember, you must add $4 to the total bet, because the table has that $5 minimum total *spread* requirement.

Betting "inside" has several other options. Instead of betting $1 straight up on a single number, you can bet $1 on a combination of any two numbers next to each other on the table layout, known as a "split," or a group-2 bet. Let's say you wish to bet the 10 and the 11, but you don't want to bet $2 total, $1 on each number. You can still bet both numbers with the $1 bet, by splitting. To "split" a bet means that you place your $1 wager on the line directly *between* the 10 and the 11. This tells the dealer that you are betting both numbers with this *single* bet. You win if either of the two numbers you selected hits. However, instead of getting paid 35:1, as you would on a single-number bet, in this case you get paid only 17:1. By increasing your odds of hitting a winner, you directly reduce the amount of your win. You may also notice that the true-odds payoff should be 17.5:1, since twice 17 = 34, and *not* 35. And 35:1 is the amount you would have won if you had selected a single-number winner. This information may be of importance to the game aficionado, but for casual play it makes little difference. On the contrary, splitting numbers can provide better opportunities for more regular winners.

For example, if we continue the betting situation I described above, the table at which you are playing may require a minimum $5 spread, with a $1 minimum per number. Therefore, if you wanted to cover five numbers, this will cost you $5. But what if you wanted to cover ten numbers? To do this at $1 per number will cost you $10. But you can achieve this by splitting. This way you can cover five *sets of two* numbers—a total of ten numbers—and still bet only your minimum requirement of a $5 spread. So, instead of betting that you will hit any one of the five numbers out of a possible thirty-eight, you now have ten numbers. This increases your chance of hitting a winner. Yes, your payoff is smaller, but you are still only risking $5 to win $17, and you double your chances of getting the $17 winner.

Grouping your numbers can be done in a variety of ways. You can also bet any combination of four numbers. To do this, place your bet on the table layout on the *corner* of the four numbers you wish to cover. This can be done on any four numbers, as long as these numbers form a square on the table layout. For instance, the numbers 10, 11, 13, and 14 form such a square on the table layout. To cover these four numbers with a single $1 bet, all you have to do is place your $1 bet directly in the center of the square, where the lines meet. If you do this with your $5 minimum spread bet, you now cover 5 times four numbers, $1 on each group of four, for a total of twenty numbers. Again you increase your chances of winning, but now your payback is down to 8:1, meaning you can at best expect only an $8 return for your $5 bet. To calculate: $1 each on five groups of four numbers, each group paying 8:1, hit any group and win $8 for your $1; the other four groups lose; therefore, you invested $5 total and won $8. Your win profit is $3. Plus you get to keep that $1 on the group-four bet that won. This is not a bad way to play, since you can also double-group such quad bets. As in the above example, you can quad the 10, 11, 13, and 14, and also quad the 7, 8, 10, and 11. In this way the 10 and the 11 ride on both quads. If either 10 or 11 hits, you win your bet twice. You can also progress to a group of six numbers in the same manner. To do this you place your $1 bet at the "T" point on the layout, in the area closest to you. This is the same as placing the quad bet, but now you are covering a total of six numbers. Again, as in our example, you can cover a group of six numbers that are immediately next to each other on the table layout, such as 7, 8, 9, 10, 11, and 12, and pay 5:1 if any of the six numbers picked is hit. This can be done for any combination of six numbers, *as long as these groups are together on the table layout.* Perhaps the most popular group bet, aside from the quad bet, is the row of three. To bet any row of three means you place your bet halfway across the line of the number nearest you without touching any other lines or numbers with your chip. This signifies that you have bet the row of three numbers immediately in line with your chip. For example: 10, 11, and 12. If any of these numbers hit, you will be paid 11:1.

On the inside bets, you can also bet the 0 and 00, either straight up, a group of two, or you can make one of only three possible group-3 bets that include the two house numbers. The most popular is what's called a "basket bet." You place your chip between the 0 and 00 on the line a little above the number 2. By doing this you have bet these three numbers: 0, 00, and 2. You can also do this by betting 0, 1, and 2, or 00, 2, and 3. These bets are the same as any group-3 bet that is placed in single-line sequence on the table layout, and also pays 11:1.

A curiosity of roulette is the group-5 bet. There is only one possible way to do this, and that is to place your chip on the corner of the 0 and 1, to cover the five numbers—0, 00, 1, 2, and 3. I call this a curiosity because it is the only such bet that can be made on roulette, and because it is curious to see anyone betting on it. It pays 6:1, but this is below the true odds. The house edge on this one bet is a whopping 7.89 percent! Since roulette does not pay fractions, you don't get nearly good enough odds to back it this way. You'll be better off backing any of the splits, group-3 bets, or placing all five numbers straight up.

Betting 0 and 00

Since the game of roulette allows you to bet on the "house" numbers, many players treat this as a safety bet—a kind of insurance, known in gambling language as a "hedge." Let's say that you have quite a few bets riding on the inside. If you don't back the 0 and 00, and the ball lands in either one of these two house numbers, all your bets lose. It is for this reason that a lot of heavy roulette players will back the 0 and 00, either singly or as a split, in proportion to the bets they have outstanding on the inside. If, for example, you have $10 at risk on inside bets, in any combination, by placing an extra $1 bet on the split between 0 and 00 you are in effect buying yourself a $17 insurance. Should either of these house numbers hit, all your bets lose, except this bet on the split between 0 and 00. Practically speaking, however, making this bet is about as good as betting insurance in blackjack. It has little bearing on your overall chances of winning, and you are better served to treat these two house numbers like any other number on the wheel. The probability of either 0 or 00 hitting is exactly the same as any of the other numbers. Nonetheless, if you spot a short-term trend toward these house numbers, betting into them is just as smart as betting into any other short-term trend.

How to Bet Outside Bets

The "outside" bets are bets in an area, and on combinations, other than any bets, or group of bets, on the numbers 1 through 36 and 0 and 00. On the table layout, this area is defined by its descriptions, which are painted on the table layout, and can be spotted easily because this is the area closest to the player as he or she sits opposite the main pit. Outside bets are as follows:

- First 12, second 12, and third 12, in squares, known as "dozens"
- First 12, second 12, and third 12, in rows (betting area opposite the 0 and 00 at what's called the "bottom" of the table layout), known as "columns"
- The numbers 1 to 18
- Even
- Red and black
- Odd
- The numbers 19 to 36

Betting the first 12 means you are betting the table layout in a square, covering the numbers 1 through 12, inclusive. Betting the second 12 numbers is covering 13 through 24, inclusive, and the third 12 covers 25 through 36. You can also make this bet in rows as a "column bet." If you do that, the first 12 will cover the numbers 1, 4, 7, 10, 13, 16, 19, 22, 25, 28, 31, and 34. Second 12 will cover the row of numbers directly next to the first row, and the third 12 will cover the last row, beginning with 3 at the top and ending with 36 at the bottom. Each of these group-12 bets pays 2:1. These are the only outside bets that pay odds. All the rest are even-money bets.

Betting "outside" usually allows higher maximum amounts. For example, if the table minimum is $5, the maximum bet inside may be a total of $2,500, with a $100 straight up bet cap, meaning you can only put a maximum of $100 on any single number, up to a total of $2,500 in any inside bet combination. Outside bets will usually have the same table minimum bet requirement, say $5, but will allow up to double the inside bet maximum, or $5,000 per our example. This means you can bet up to $5,000 on any outside bet combination, or any single outside bet. Most often these high limits are played by high rollers, and these people will mostly bet either the red or the black. As far as odds of winning go, they might as well bet odd or even, or any of the other even-money outside bets. In all cases, players of American roulette, which employs both the 0 and 00, are giving up a house edge percentage of 5.26 percent.

European Roulette Rules and the En-Prison Rule

European roulette is played on a single-zero wheel and also features a favorable "en prison" rule. Under this rule if you make any even-money bet—such as on red, black, odd, even, 1-to-18, and/or 19-to-36—and the ball lands on the zero house number, you now have the option of either asking for half of your bet back, or leaving it en-prison—meaning, in French, that the bet is "imprisoned." If an imprisoned bet wins on the next spin, it is released and the player gets it back, *without winnings.* There is, however, a difference of rules among some European casinos concerning what happens to the en-prison bet if the house zero is repeated while the en-prison bet is so held. In some European casinos, half of the even money bet is returned if the ball lands on the house zero consecutively, while the player's en-prison bet is so held. The house edge on this is 1.36 percent. At other casinos, if a house zero landed again on the second spin while the original bet was en-prison, the bet lost. In some such casinos, you can ask the dealer to move that imprisoned bet to another wager before the next spin. The house edge on this version of the en-prison bet is 1.39 percent. At other casinos, the rule is that if two zeros occur in a row while the original bet is en-prison, then the bet becomes "double imprisoned." In this case *two* winning bets in a row must occur to release it (precisely which two winning bets isn't clear). If anything else occurs, including more zeros, the bet is lost. The house edge on this version is 1.31 percent. On most of these games, however, there is also a kind of "surrender" option available, and that is to ask the dealer to return half the bet to you before any more spins. This is the thing to do, of course. In most other casinos, the standard en-prison rule simply means that the bet remains en-prison until a non-zero event happens, in which case it is returned if the winner was the player's bet, or lost if the player's bet was not the winning event. The house edge on this version is 1.36 percent.

Atlantic City En-Prison Rules

In Atlantic City, on specified games, all even money bets—such as on red, black, odd, even, 1-to-18, and/or 19-to-36—play to a variation of the European en-prison rule. If the ball lands in 0 or 00 the player will lose only *half* of his even-money bets. This lowers the house edge to 2.63 percent on these bets. However, for some strange reason the casinos can't explain, this rule does *not* apply to their single-zero games. This is probably because the single-zero games already have a lowered house edge, from the standard 5.26 percent on the two-zero wheel, to the 2.7 percent on the single-zero wheel. Basically, this Atlantic City en-prison rule variation does only one thing: it lowers the house edge from the standard 5.26 percent on those specified bets to 2.63 percent. Therefore, when playing the two-zero game, it is better to play one that offers these bets with this rule. Otherwise, it is better to play the single-zero wheel whenever possible.

Odds, Pays, and Probabilities

Roulette can be classified into three distinct groups, by rules: American rules, European rules, and Atlantic City rules. American rules are the standard in most U.S. casinos, and I have referred to them in this book as American roulette. Similarly, the European rules are those for the game I described as European roulette, or as single-zero roulette—although the better differentiation would be to classify them by the use of the "en-prison" rule, which some American single-zero roulette rules use, and others don't, while several European casinos play that rule differently. The Atlantic City rules are an oddity; they use a variation on the European en-prison rule, but apply it only to the American two-zero roulette. It is *not* available on their version of the single-zero game. Yes, I realize that this is kind of confusing, but the confusion stems from the availability of so many variations to the basic roulette rules, and the flexibility that these variations allow. For a game that really isn't all that popular anymore, it certainly offers a variety of options. I will now again turn to my fellow columnist and mathematical genius, Michael Shackleford, the Wizard of Odds. With the assistance of his analysis of the game's odds and probabilities, I offer you the following chart that describes the various events in the game of American roulette.

American Roulette Pays and Probabilities

BET	PAYS	PROBABILITY (%)
Red	1:1	47.37
Black	1:1	47.37
Odd	1:1	47.37
Even	1:1	47.37

American Roulette Pays and Probabilities (cont.)

BET	PAYS	PROBABILITY (%)
1-to-18	1:1	47.37
19-to-36	1:1	47.37
1-to-12	2:1	31.58
13-to-24	2:1	31.58
25-to-36	2:1	31.58
Columns of 12	2:1	31.58
Straight up bet	35:1	2.63
Group-2 bets (splits)	17:1	5.26
Group-3 bets (lines)	11:1	7.89
Group-4 bets (quads)	8:1	10.53
Group-6 bets (blocks)	5:1	15.79
0, 00, 1,2,3, group-5 bet	6:1	13.16

Simple Strategy

Although popularized in films and fiction, roulette, as played in America, is almost universally considered by players to be the sucker's game. Powerful arguments can be made to support this view, but they are not necessarily correct. European roulette is played only with the single 0, and this so dramatically improves the odds that the game enjoys a considerably higher degree of popularity. While American roulette hits the player with a 5.26 percent disadvantage, European roulette has only a 2.7 percent edge in favor of the house. This means a lot both in short-term and long-term betting strategy. Lately, in an effort to revitalize the game of roulette, quite a few major American casinos have begun to offer European roulette. For anyone contemplating any kind of serious play on roulette, that is the game I suggest you look for. The direct disadvantage is that European roulette offered in American casinos will normally require much higher minimum bets than American roulette with the two zeros. The reasons are obvious. Since the casinos are giving up half their advantage, they want bigger bets to offset this.

Most European roulette tables in U.S. casinos will require a minimum $5 bet, with a minimum $25 spread on the inside and a minimum $25 bet on the outside. There are variations from casino to casino, but the Bellagio, Caesars Palace, Tropicana, MGM, and Monte Carlo in Las Vegas all play the European roulette with these limits. If you plan to be a serious roulette player, with a bankroll to match, these limits should not scare you. The favorable reduction in house edge you are getting will, in the long run, make up for the higher minimum amounts required to make a bet. And if you are a high roller, you will probably bet bigger than the minimum anyway, so why stick yourself up and play the two-zero wheel? Even if you just want a casual experience with roulette, finding a single-zero wheel with lower betting limits will provide you with a better betting experience, and better odds of winning. In fact, it is my hope that all American casinos will junk the two-zero wheel altogether and play only the European roulette. This will aid revitalization efforts for this game, and offer more players more choices.

There are so many various systems to beat the roulette wheel that I'd need several hundred pages just to describe them. Likewise, there are as many players who have gone broke trying to prove their validity. In roulette, each new spin is a new and independent event. The wheel and the ball have no memory, and therefore any probability theory based on forecasting future events based on past events is bogus. There is simply no way of telling what the outcome of the next spin will be based on what past outcomes have been. And in roulette you don't even get an equal chance at it, even if you bet 50-50 propositions. At best you get a 47 percent chance of a win on any even-money bet, like red or black, with American roulette. You get better odds of 49 percent with the single-zero European wheel, but still not even. No matter which way you look at it, the casino advantage will eat you up in the long term. If you played American roulette for a whole year, twenty-four hours a day, and you made even-money bets, in the end you'd be 5.26 percent short of what you started with. So, you ask, why should I play roulette at all? The answer lies in short-term trends.

A while ago I was watching a game of roulette at Caesars Palace in Las Vegas and saw a sequence of twenty-two consecutive winners on red. This is quite unusual, but it does happen—often quite frequently and on various such possible combinations. A winning sequence of three, four, even five consecutive winners on either red or black is not that unusual, but such a long trend is. It is at such a time that betting into the trend can prove very profitable. The same applies to an observation session I had at the Rio in Las Vegas. On this particular table, out of thirty spins the 0 and 00, counted jointly, came up nine times. Again, this is an unusual occurrence, and testifies to smart play through observation. On this occasion two players at that table recognized this and pressed their bets on the 0 and 00 split. Even though they lost several spins in a row, they more than made up for it when their numbers hit. They hit again and again, for that sequence, and each player made off with a nice stack of $100 chips. I do not recommend that you favor any one number over the other, but spotting such short-term trends is the only advantage roulette players have. In fact, several theories by other well-known gaming experts testify to the validity of observant play and maximizing your bets into short-term trends.

The same strategy would apply if you spotted a biased

wheel—a wheel whose perfectly accurate balance has been somehow compromised. Since all major gaming centers regularly check the accuracy of their games, such occurrences are rare and do not last long. Perhaps this particular wheel was bumped, or the wood settled or reacted to atmospheric changes. If you see that the wheel you are playing is hitting a specific area and specific numbers contrary to equal probability, you have either spotted a short-term trend or are playing a biased wheel. In either case the smart roulette player will alter her betting strategy and bet into this trend or into the biased area.

A lot of people employ the simplest system of all: the double-up system, also known as the Martingale system. This simple system calls for a player to double his bet each time he loses. The theory goes that, no matter what the short-term trend, eventually that player will hit a winner and recover all his bets, plus the profit of his original betting unit. Theoretically, this is fine. However, it would not be unusual to see such a player betting $50,000 to win $5, with the $5 being his original even-money bet. Sounds ridiculous? It is, especially since in any casino you will find table limits. Therefore if you did employ such a ludicrous system, you could quickly find yourself at the table limit, without any hope of ever recovering your bets, much less find yourself in profit. Systems that attempt to overcome the long-term house edge, and attempt to create some kind of future forecast based on past events, all lead to inevitable disaster. But an observant player *can* use a betting progression to increase his short-term win potential by betting into an existing short-term trend. Even if you were to toss a coin in the air, it is not unusual to see it come up heads several times in a row. This is a short-term trend. Eventually, if you continued to toss the coin, the outcome would turn out almost even (fractionally more "tails" than "heads," because on U.S. coins the head side contains more metal and is, therefore, a tiny bit heavier, resulting in the head side landing head down with tails up a few tenths of a percentage point more frequently—as a result, a coin toss even in laboratory statistical tests is not an even proposition, as long as you use the specified U.S. Mint currency coins; coins from other countries will work out differently).

In roulette, such short-term trends can produce several black hits in a row, or red, or even, or odd, even a series of specific numbers, as in the two stories I told earlier. If this happens, and you see it happening and you recognize it is happening, increasing your bets works to your advantage. However, unlike the double-up systems, here you are increasing your bets *when you are winning,* and *not* when you are losing. Simply put, this means you are not chasing your money.

This applies to any gambling game: when you are winning, bet more, because you are betting with *their* money, not yours, and if you continue to win, you'll clean up. In roulette this principle is crucial, because any other way of playing will make you a loser in the long run. But there is still luck. Yes, you can be lucky, against all odds. I saw a young man at the Las Vegas Hilton a few years ago walk up to a roulette table and place a $100 chip straight up on the number 10. It hit and he won $3,500! That was pure luck. It happens, and in roulette it happens comparatively often. It just depends on whether the gods smile on you at that particular time and all the stars are right, and whatever else is necessary to make you so lucky. But for any kind of consistent play at roulette, consider the following hints:

- Play *only* the European one-zero roulette *if* you can find it. If you can't find it, make the best of the American roulette with one or more of the options listed here.

- Bet the first 12, second 12 or third 12, either in square groups, or the columns. Any winner will pay 2:1. Bet any two of these combinations, and if you hit, you make a profit of one unit for each two you bet. For example, if you bet $5 each on the first and second 12, leaving the third 12 open, and you hit a winner on the second 12, your first 12 bet will lose, but your second 12 bet will pay you 2:1, or $10. So, you risked a total of $10, and won $10, but you also got to keep that $5 bet in that dozen where you won, so you made a $5 profit, for a gross of $15. You can then press your winner with the extra $5, let that ride, and if it hits again, you have now won $20 for a gross of $30 and a $10 win, with a total capital risk of only $10 of your own money over these two spins.
- Bet group-4 bets, and group these together to double up on the common numbers. Let's say you bet a group-4 of 1, 2, 4, and 5. You can then also bet another group-4 with 2, 3, 5, and 6. This gives you the 2 and the 5 as your common numbers. If these hit, you get paid twice. You can advance this still further by betting another group, say 4, 5, 7, and 8. This will give you a "three-way 5," and "two-way 4 and 5," and "2 and 5," and so on.
- Bet splits instead of straight up numbers, or bet any straight up number with splits on either side of it. For example, straight up on "11," and splits on "11 and 8," "11 and 14," "11 and 10," and "11 and 12." Your 11 is the common number, and if it hits you get paid 35:1 on the 11, and 17:1 on the other four splits that had 11 as the common number. And, of course, if the 11 does not hit, but any of the other numbers you split it with do, you still get 17:1.
- Never bet just straight up numbers with no splits or groups to go with them. Even if you covered *all* the

possible numbers—thirty-eight on American roulette and thirty-seven on the European wheel—you'd still be paid only 35:1, and therefore come out a loser. If you bet any straight up numbers, also bet some splits and groups around them.

- Offset your groups. This means to group your bets over different areas of the board. If you bet groups at the top of the table layout, top being the first eighteen, also bet a similar group at the other end of the layout. Remember, the wheel *does not* have the numbers grouped in the same sequence as they are shown on the table layout. By offsetting your groups, you increase your chances of winning.
- Remember how much you are betting. If you bet $38, and your chances of *any single or combination win* are less than the amount you bet, you are a loser before the game even begins. So remember the value of your gaming chips, remember how many you bet and where, and *calculate* what your win potential is *before* you make the bets.
- If you win, press your bet, but don't blow it all on the next spin. Try to play with the money you won, and keep the money you bought in with. This way you are likely to feel better about bigger bets and give yourself a chance for bigger wins if you hit again. If you lose, go back to your minimum bet and start over.
- Watch for short-term trends. If you spot one, whatever it is, bet into it immediately and continue to bet into it and press your bets as long as it lasts. But remember that trends can be as little as two in a row, or as long as fate can make them. Don't push it if it's not there.
- If you have the money, bet the even-money bets in as large amounts as your bankroll can take. And watch out for those short-term trends. As in my earlier example, if you were a bettor on red, and saw the

twenty-two straight reds trend, you would have made a ton of cash. If you see such a trend, bet it, but if you see it going away, then *you* go away too. It won't come back just because you want it to, or because you are trying to coax it back with silly bets.

The best advice I can give you for roulette is the same as for Craps: Get in, make your money, and get out. Any prolonged exposure to the game of roulette will *inevitably* lead you to lose money. *But* if you're smart, observant, and know how to bet into the short-term trends you recognize, you can make as much in thirty minutes of play as you could ever hope to make by grinding out small percentages over long periods of time, as dictated by a few poor souls still plugging roulette systems. For those readers who wish to make a more detailed study of roulette, and discover some more detailed strategies and playing methods, I refer you to my book *Powerful Profits: Winning Strategies for Casino Games.*

Some Roulette Ramblings

There are a few observations that I wanted to add to this chapter on roulette, but that didn't fit very well within the explanation of the game, and how to play it. In all my chapters I try to strike a balance between informative and interesting, but usually the game requires that we first concentrate on the informative and only later, if we have the space, talk a little more about some of the more interesting aspects of the game. One such item of potential interest has to do with the single-zero roulette. Although, as I have explained, this is the better alternative (often called European roulette in order to differentiate between it and the American version with two house numbers, 0 and 00), where can you play it, other than in Europe?

Well, in the United States, the single-zero wheel can be found in several of the upper-echelon casinos in Las Vegas and Atlantic City alike. I classify these casinos as "upper echelon" because most of them are among the more expensive resorts, and these single-zero games traditionally require much higher wagering limits. These higher limits are usually only possible for players whose bankrolls can withstand it, and these players are traditionally found among more posh casino resorts. The bread-and-butter brigades of ordinary folk are mostly limited to the higher-house-edge 0 and 00 wheels, which provide much lower betting requirements. The caviar class may enjoy the lower-house-edge single-zero wheel, but they are made to pay more for it. So, you see, in the final tally it's really a fair trade-off. Those who can afford to spend more get a slightly better game, while those who have less to spend get a game that's slightly less lucrative, but much more accessible. In the end, remember that roulette is one of the premier house games and that—mathematically speaking—the house edge is constant. So, even though the perhaps more "privileged" class of high-rolling players may get a single-zero game, they are still playing a game whose house edge is a constant 2.7 percent. Don't feel too bad if you aren't a member of the Millionaire's Club. Just remember that the $1 slots you play usually only hold 2 percent for the house, so you're actually a smarter player than they are!

But roulette isn't the ogre of casino games that it is usually made out to be. Although when we look at the game from the mathematical perspective, we do find that the 5.26 percent house edge on the 0 and 00 wheel, and the 2.7 percent house edge on the single-zero wheel, are not conducive to the inclusion of this game among the better casino games odds-wise for your investment, the truth is that even games with a high house edge have to pay off. A slot machine that holds 20 percent for the house—which many do—still has to pay out 80 percent. So, a game like roulette that holds either the 5.26 percent or the 2.7 percent for the house also means that it will pay out 94.74 percent and 97.30 percent, respectively. That's a pretty good payback percentage, especially when compared with many of the other casino games, including slot machines. Nevertheless, just as game selection is important in the overall professionalism of a casino gambler, it is also important in roulette. Though you may not wish to be a professional gambler, you can learn, and practice, the principles of good game selection and the criteria for such decisions. Although many of the single-zero roulette games are only offered in the "premium" casino resorts, and at tables whose overall spread may require more money than is viable for your budget, there are quite a few casinos that offer the single-zero wheel at much lower overall bet requirements. Many of these casinos will actually offer the single-zero game with only a total $25 minimum required spread, or $25 on any single inside or outside bet. This is not too bad, especially when you consider that you are getting more than 50 percent better odds on this game than on the alternative 0 and 00 wheels. Yes, many of these casinos will require a $100 spread, but some that do offer this lower $25 spread—actually lower it even further at specific times.

For example, if you can play in Las Vegas in midweek, such as Monday through Thursday, you are quite likely to find some of the better roulette games at $10 or $15 spread requirements, a substantially lower mark than the $25 that most such single-zero games will usually command. Playing in the wee hours of the morning, say from 3:00 A.M. to about 7:00 A.M., may also provide you with this better game at a lower overall spread and minimum wager requirements. If you wish to play roulette and you are able to do just a little bit of advance planning and perhaps some research, you may be able to get a better game and thus give yourself a more rewarding and profitable experience. So, here is a list of casinos in Las Vegas and Atlantic City that provide the single-zero roulette game:

Las Vegas single-zero roulette

Aladdin
Bellagio
Luxor
Mandalay Bay
Mirage
Monte Carlo
Nevada Palace
Stratosphere
Tropicana
Venetian

The Nevada Palace, a small casino on the Boulder Strip, often offers this game for as low as 10 cents per bet, with a small spread requirement (which can vary, depending on the day and time of the game). The Bellagio has limits of $100 that are pretty much standard, while the Mirage has $25 to $50 limits on this game. Also, both the Mirage and Bellagio play a version of the European en-prison rule, with a half-bet back, and this can lower the house edge even further, to about 1.36 percent.

Atlantic City single-zero roulette

Bally's Park Place
Caesars
Harrah's
Hilton
Sands
Showboat
Taj Majal
Tropicana
Trump Marina

In addition to these, two Midwest casinos offer this single-zero wheel—the Grand Tunica in Mississippi and the Grand Victoria in Lawrenceburg, Indiana. Other casinos may offer these games from time to time, depending on how much they want to promote the game of roulette, and how much they wish to attract customers. When casinos that normally don't offer the single-zero wheel suddenly start to advertise or publicize it, they are using this as a marketing and promotional tool. If the remainder of the game's rules and options remain unaffected, by all means play this game, even in those casinos where it is not likely to remain as the main staple of their game mix. While the promotion runs, exploit it to your advantage, but always be mindful of the possible changes to the various rules of the game that may have somehow been subtly introduced. It doesn't take much to turn what is essentially a not-too-bad game into one that is truly a monster. I think that if you have understood what I've written in this chapter, and what I also discussed in the chapter on roulette in my book *Powerful Profits: Winning Strategies for Casino Games,* then you will be able to make good and informed choices for yourself.

Some Thoughts on Systems

In most of my books I take the time to differentiate between what is a gambling "system" and what is a "method." "System" used to mean a viable playing *strategy,* such as card counting in blackjack. Unfortunately, over the years the word "system" has become corrupted by the many various get-rich-quick schemes for gamblers. Although the word system was meant to show a sound wagering method, it has come to mean something sleazy, or something that's "not really a good deal." Many writers still use the word system when describing either a strategy or a method, because these distinctions have not been properly made. To my mind, something like the traditional Martingale or the Super Martingale systems are the perfect example of why the word system has come to mean something bogus. If you don't know what a Martingale system is, I refer you to my book on winning strategies, in which I describe it and show why it doesn't work. Here, suffice it to say that when we understand roulette from within the mathematical model, the fact remains that the Law of Large Numbers will prevail, and that the more you play the closer you will get to the number constant. Simply put, the ball has no memory, and therefore each spin is an independent event. Consequently, any system that relies on previous events as somehow being able to influence future events, or have some sort of an impact on them, is and has to be bogus. Thousands of such "systems" are being sold all over the world. They used to arrive by direct mail; now they are sold via the Internet, through hundreds of websites. These systems are all a version of doubling-your-bet progressions, and all basically rely on the assumption that independent events are somehow linked and interconnected, and that therefore there are ways of defeating the games regardless of the facts of the math.

In the early years of the twentieth century, a man who played roulette in Monte Carlo "broke the bank," and he was hailed as the only player ever to devise a roulette system for beating the game. What actually happened is that he just got really lucky and had no system at all. It was one of those statistical anomalies allowed for in numbers theory. Nevertheless, this event began the current trend in the selling of various gambling systems, and that's what has corrupted the meaning of the word. In fact, some encyclopedias call these kinds of systems the Monte Carlo fallacy.

I discuss this in detail in my book *Powerful Profits: Winning Strategies for Casino Games,* wherein I also take further issue with the distinction between a "system" and what I now prefer to call a sound strategy—namely a "method." I am, however, also not necessarily in agreement with the pure mathematicians and statisticians. You see, the problem is that this Law of Large Numbers, or any of the so-called mathematical laws of anything, or any of the principles upon which mathematicians base their analysis of events, are fundamentally flawed. While the Law of Large Numbers works nicely within the domain of the theory, and is perfectly suited for programming into a computer for the purpose of providing computerized test results, the problem is that *the theory is being tested by the same principles that led to the theory.* In other words, the mathematicians have all decided to agree that they will call certain events, say, an "apple"—for the sake of an example that most of us can understand—and that, therefore, all events of this kind will be called "apple." Furthermore, they have agreed that the test for what is, or is not, an "apple" will be another apple. So, they test other things by the apple test. If it is an apple, they test it with another apple, and lo and behold the result is an apple. Voilà! A proof! Well, not quite. You see, those that make mathematics of gambling out to be the sole and only answer, the holy grail by which all gambling play should be undertaken, forget that they are only a clan that has agreed to call something by a certain label, and then they test it with itself. A mathematical argument that a game's "constant" is X percent, which is subsequently "proved" by compiling a computer program as a means of playing a billion events and then compare the results, forgets that the very same mathematics was used to program the test. Therefore, they are trying to prove that an apple is an apple by comparing it with another apple and using that second apple as a verification of the first apple. All fine and good, as long as you agree that these "things" are going to be called "apples," and that, therefore, their verification by themselves from within themselves and to themselves will provide the test and proof.

As long as you live within the "box" where everybody agrees that all apples are apples, and that the test of the validity of the apple is if it *is* an apple, then you're fine. But all that tells you is this: If it is an apple, therefore it is an apple. Furthermore, to test this assertion, the mathematicians use the apple to program a machine with the same set of presuppositions to test the apple by the fact that it is an apple. What has this done? Well, it proved that (a = a)—blue equals blue; apple equals apple; red equals red—and so on. However, none of this tells us precisely what an apple *is,* or what "red" *is,* or what "blue" *is,* or what the reality of these "things" actually is. All we have achieved is to learn that as long as we agree that these "things" are going to be called "numbers" and that they will form "patterns" as we agreed and as long as we agree that these will "mean" something on which we also agree, then we have a formula that can be programmed into a computer. And as long as these "laws" remain in our agreement, and are used by themselves to program the machine to churn them out and verify them, we will always come up with some kind of an absolute— and that's what we call the "Laws of Mathematics," or "Laws of Nature," or the "Law of Large Numbers." Unfortunately, none of this actually tells us anything, other than that the formulas will work as long as we all agree that they will work. Proving that an apple is an apple by showing us another apple does nothing more than show that we have a whole lot more to learn before we even begin to understand the truth of what and where we actually are.

I call this kind of thinking the "omnipotent ignorance syndrome." All of empirical science and mathematics are infected with it. This is the same kind of thinking that led earlier human beings to believe that the world was flat, that the sun moved around the earth instead of the other way around, and that people who invent telescopes are heretics and must be burned at the stake. The so-called science of our world is nothing more than a consensus, an agreement, among the vast majority of like-thinking human beings, that what we think we see will be called "that," and given that label from this point on. And so this gets taught to children, who then teach it to their children, and so on, and pretty soon we have textbooks that hold this to be some kind of a self-evident truth, and no more thinking should be involved. Students are asked to simply learn it and then regurgitate it during exams, upon which they get a diploma, which is kind of like a stamp that says "You're in the club— now you think like us." And so the world goes on, merrily happy in its ignorance, while the mathematicians spin their webs of numbers and think they are actually providing a window to the truth. What they are actually doing is merely putting up a signpost to what "may" be up ahead. A useful guide, but not the answer—no matter how much they would like to claim it to be.

What is most damaging about this, and particularly so to strategy play in casino games, is the overwhelming sense of superiority and self-importance that math gurus have, and would like us to admire. Mathematicians who write about, analyze, or comment on casino games and their strategies or methods of play feel uniquely empowered with some "secret" truths, or knowledge. Not so. They are merely skilled and intelligent people who have mastered *one form of possible* understanding, and provided a signpost for what *may* be. They do not, however, have the answer to what actually *is*.

I have provided this brief commentary on a deep subject, one fraught with much conjecture and positional analysis. There are no absolutes, and no hard-and-fast answers. Mathematics of casino games is one way of learning to understand, but there are other means of understanding. They are the human elements—and these, by their very nature, cannot be mathematically identifiable or numerically programmable. Therefore, no computer test of any strategy or method can be truly accurate, because no such test will, or can, allow for the human factors that can't be numerically quantified or exponentiated. As a result, there are many sound methods of play possible, even if—perhaps—the math shows otherwise. It so shows only because the math itself, and the tests so used, is limited to quantification, and not, therefore, representative of the whole. And that's the fallacy of mathematics in strategies.

Needless to say, I am preparing myself for an onslaught of criticism for this position. Most people simply will not understand the concept of "open mind," nor will they allow for the supposition that the world may not actually be exactly what they think it is. This is a problem that I have faced many times, and usually with mathematicians, or persons for whom such thinking forms the very core of understanding of their being and their universe.

People who live in a box where everyone thinks the same way usually don't *know* that they are in a box; they have no concept of what "box," "inside," or "outside" means in relation to them. Consequently, trying to offer any form of enlightenment is like trying to describe color to a person who is blind. We can do this if we translate the "color" into a "spectrum," which then can be quantified and enumerated, and exponentiated and then rendered in physical form as a representation that the person can then comprehend through tactile means, but this is still only a small step. It does nothing to explain the joy of the hue of a sunrise, the color of the silvery clouds, or the beauty of a rainbow. All it does is show what is, essentially, a bunch of numbers—numbers that "kind of" represent what the color "kind of" is—but, well, it really isn't. But, that's the best we can do at this time for the person who is blind and for those in the box. Until those inside that box allow for at least the possibility that there could be something more than they think there is, the best we can do is to show the rainbow as a bunch of numbers.

But one day the box will break, the mind and eyes will open, and the whole will be known.

What does this have to do with casino games or methods and strategies? Well, think of it this way: next time you read something, or hear someone who talks about odds and percentages and says something like, "No strategies that are offered for mathematically negative expectation games can or will work," remember that this is a person who is disabled, one whose mind is closed, one who lives inside a box where only others who think like him live. This person has not mastered the reality of the universe; he has merely mastered the consensus among others of his kind who think like him and who have all agreed that they will label certain things in a certain way. Find them useful as the bearers of a lantern along your way toward the understanding of viable and profit-generating strategies, but pity them also for seeing only the numbers and not seeing the rainbow.

Live Poker—Texas Hold'Em

Casino live poker is the only game in which the house—the casino—does not participate. This means that live poker is the only table game that is not a "house-banked" game. In all other casino table games, you are playing against the casino, but in live poker you are playing directly against the other players. The casino merely facilitates the game, providing the room, tables, chairs, dealers, personnel, services, and so on—but the casino is not directly involved in the actual game. For this reason, many budget-minded corporate executives who control most of today's casinos are against keeping this game as part of the mainstream casino table games. Since the casino doesn't participate in the game, it can't alter it to assure itself of a win by changing the payoffs to pay at less than the true odds, as is the case in all other casino table games. Various alterations to their games' rules—such as paying off at less-than-true odds—are what casinos do in all other table games to assure themselves of a steady percentage "win" over each game over the long term. This is how casinos make profits, and how and why they can continue to stay in business. This is what constitutes the "house edge" on these games. Without that the casinos would be unable to stay in business, and players would have nowhere to play.

The corporate bean counters in modern casinos don't like live poker because it is labor intensive, requiring a lot of "people" time, and that costs money. People need to be fed and clothed, they get sick, they move on, they need to be supervised, hired and fired, and so on. The costs of the benefits and health care, and all that other stuff, simply make people the most expensive item of any casino's daily operational expense. Little wonder that the casinos try to eliminate the need for labor-intensive games and services as much as possible. There is yet another "killer" in how casino corporations see live poker—the floor space it occupies. An average four-table poker room takes up about the same space as the two largest rooms in an average house— about 1,200 square feet. Larger rooms take up much more. If you want to check out one of the biggest poker rooms in Las Vegas, go to the Bellagio. You'll quickly learn not only how expensive it gets to run a room like that, but also how much floor space it requires. For a large casino like the Bellagio, this isn't as much of a problem. But for the smaller casinos— Arizona Charlie's, for example—there are only two tables in an area the size of a small living room. Therefore, the smaller the casino, the more attention has to be paid to the cost per square foot.

Of course, the big casinos also take this into account, and here's why: In a casino floor area of about 1,000 square feet, the casino can easily install up to fifty slot machines. Each of these machines will average a drop of about $1,500 per month, and that means that the casino will realize a drop of about $75,000 per month from that area. Now, consider if that area is occupied instead by a four-table poker room. Each table will drop about $1,000 in a twenty-four-hour period, provided, of course, that there are enough players to play on all four tables all the time. If this were so, each of these four tables would make about $30,000 per month for the casino, and that would be $120,000 per month over all the tables. So far so good—but, most of the time, the tables will only be half full, or only two will be in action some of the time, and mostly not "24/7" as the slot machines are. Generally, only one table will play around the clock, or most of the time, say twenty hours a day, while the others will only be in action about eight hours per day, or less. On average, therefore, among the four tables, the drop will be only $2,000 per day, which is $60,000 per month. You can see the difference—putting slots in that same space will result in the casino averaging $75,000 per month, and that is pretty much assured because the machines will make this as long as they are played. Thus, by getting rid of the poker room, the casinos will save the cost of wages for thirty or so employees, and all of their benefits, and will lose the necessity of additional supervisory and surveillance department staff and the requirements for gaming taxes on the tables. They are able to get rid of the equipment, services, and so on—well, you get the picture. It turns out that slots will not only result in about $15,000 per month more for the casino in the same space as the four-table poker room, but will also "save" the casino about another $100,000 per month in various other costs, such as wages, benefits, equipment, extra personnel, and operational maintenance. Little wonder why corporate executives in many smaller casinos, as well as many large ones, really don't like live poker at all.

Live poker makes money for the casino by what's called the "rake," and that is a "fee"—that becomes the "drop"—charged by the casino from each pot by a specified percentage, with a stated maximum cap. For example, most Seven-Card Stud games in casino poker rooms have a sign that says what the game is, what limits are being played, and what the rake is. This rake is the percentage amount charged by the casino and taken from each pot to pay for facilitating the game. That amount so taken from each pot is dropped by the dealer into a special collection box beneath the table, and that money then becomes the casino's drop for that table and, hence, its gross receipts for providing the game and the facilities. The actual amounts of the percentage so withheld from each pot depend on the game and the casino. Las Vegas casino poker rooms usually charge a 10 percent rake on Seven-Card Stud games, with a $4.50 maximum. This means that the casino will take from each pot 10 percent of all the money wagered by all players in that one hand, up to the maximum amount of $4.50. Thus, if the size of the pot reaches $45 total, by that point the casino has already collected its maximum 10 percent, which is $4.50. If the pot becomes bigger thereafter, no additional rake is charged and, therefore, any wagers over and above that raked maximum are free from further charge by the casino rake. Of course, if the size of the pot is less than $45, as in this example, then the casino still takes the rake, usually in increments of 5 percent, and in 25 cent increments. So, for example, a pot with $38 in it would be raked by the casino in 5 percent increments, and that would be to the nearest lowest whole-dollar amount as able to be raked with the use of quarters, in this case $3.75—because the actual 10 percent would have been $3.80. There are no coins or chips used in any casino that are of less value than 25 cents, so the nearest 5 percent incremental rake charge here comes to $3.75.

In Texas Hold'Em games, the rake is usually only 5 percent, with a maximum of only $3 in most of the regular games. This is one of the reasons why Texas Hold'Em is not only the better game, but is far superior to any other game, particularly Seven-Card Stud. Casinos know that most people are at least a little familiar with Seven-Card Stud, since most people have played something like it in home games, and therefore they spread the game in the casino but make sure they charge their maximum rake early—that's why the 10 percent charge is so deadly. Most of the time, if you want to play Seven-Card Stud in the casino poker rooms, you will be much better off playing at the $5–$10 games and higher, because the standard $1–$4 or $1–$5 games are a killer on the bankroll, mostly because of this 10 percent house rake. Given the bring-in rules for Seven-Card Stud, the side rakes for jackpots and such, the tips and other costs of the game, if you are playing a $1–$5 game you will need to make $65 per hour just to break even. That's how deadly these games are with a 10 percent rake. However, the same game at the $5–$10 table limits and higher usually have only a 5 percent rake, with a $3 maximum. That's because casinos know that only casual players usually play the small $1–$5 and $1–$4 games, while the more knowledge-able players play in these higher games. Of course, the higher the game, the more times the casino will be able to rake the maximum, and that's also why the rake is tradition-ally lower in the higher-limit poker games. Texas Hold 'Em is the exception, where the pots are usually bigger even in the small $4–$8 games, and therefore the rake is usually only 5 percent with a $3 maximum. The exception to this are lower-limit games such as $2–$4 games, where the 10 percent rake usually applies, at a $4.50 and even $5 maxi-mum. These games are usually just as bad for you as the small limit Seven-Card Stud games, and for the same reasons.

Live poker is the best game to play in any casino. There is a very simple reason for this, and if you haven't already guessed, here it is: live poker is the only casino game where you are *not* playing against the casino. It's that simple. Because the casino doesn't play, it can't change the game or pay off at less-than-true odds. Therefore, you are not fighting any house edge. In fact, there is *no house edge* in live poker. Although the rake could be called a "cost" of the game, it isn't a house edge, in the same sense as the other games are understood. For this simple reason, live poker is a beatable game. You are playing against the other players. Therefore, your abilities, knowledge, and skills directly influence your outcome and your profitability. Furthermore, live poker is also a *dependent* game—just as blackjack but without the house edge—because what cards are yet to be dealt in any round of dealing are directly dependent on the cards that have already been dealt. Unlike games like Craps or roulette, for example, in which the toss of the dice or the roll of the number are all independent events, having no memory of past results, in any one round of dealing in any poker game, the cards that are yet to be dealt are directly dependent on those that have already been dealt. This means that you, as a skilled player, can actually detect and calculate with a fair degree of accuracy your odds of having the winning hand. You can do this if your calculation is based on an analysis of the mathematical probabilities of the possible events and on the knowledge you gain from observing which cards have already been dealt, and which cards, therefore, still have the possibility *of being* dealt, as this applies to your hand and the cards you may still need, or those that your opponents could potentially use to make their hands better. All this information is available in live poker, and you can use it to make determinations and decisions that directly affect your profits and losses.

Although mastering live poker, and the various poker games, takes a lot more knowledge and skill than just these examples, the point I am making is that in live poker you are the master of your destiny—you, and only you, have the power to make decisions that will result in your being a winner or a loser. For these reasons, live poker is the game of choice for most professional gamblers, and certainly the main choice for the many more semiprofessional gamblers, people who play for profit regularly but have other forms of supplementary income. True poker professionals—those whose actual income is directly derived from poker and only poker—usually play in the big-money tournaments, such as the World Series of Poker in Las Vegas, the World Poker Tour, or many of the other national and international poker tournaments. Many of these have a buy-in requirement of $10,000, $25,000, or even more, and are therefore the domain of true poker professionals. Live poker is the game of choice among those players who are dedicated to winning money.

Many books are available for you to choose from, to learn about any and all of the live poker games that are available in major casinos and other venues, such as the popular card room casinos where only poker games, and poker-type table games, are offered. These poker card rooms are located throughout California, and many more in the various other tribal gaming centers throughout the United States, as well as in many countries around the world. Live poker has justifiably become one of the most universal gambling games, and I personally consider it the best casino game you will ever find or learn to play. It is, however, not my intention in *this* book to duplicate the efforts of the many fine authors of poker books. All I wish to do here is simply introduce you to the two great poker games: Texas Hold'Em and Seven-Card Stud, the two most common games you will find in all casino poker rooms and other poker card rooms. With the explosion of the Internet, you will also find many online casinos and poker rooms that offer these two games. These are the two games that you should learn first.

My offering in this book is simple and to the point. I provide the basics of the games, so that you can get to playing as quickly and as comfortably as is possible. For those readers who are interested in more in-depth analysis of these poker games, or other poker games, I would recommend that you seek out some of the many fine books written about these games, including my book *Powerful Profits from Video Poker.* They are available everywhere books are sold and especially from the Gambler's Book Shop in Las Vegas, the Gambler's General Store in Las Vegas, and in particular from a very good poker magazine called *Card Player* (www.cardplayer.com). From any of these sources you can get all the detailed poker information you require. For now, let me introduce you to the two greatest poker games in the world, beginning with my all-time favorite, Texas Hold'Em.

INTRODUCTION TO TEXAS HOLD'EM

In contemporary times, Hold'Em poker is perhaps most famous as *the* game played during the $10,000 buy-in World Series of Poker tournament held each year in Las Vegas at Binion's Horseshoe, downtown. But this poker game is not limited to high-stakes play or tournament play. It can be just as much fun—and just as profitable—as part of your regular casino playing fare. So, in this chapter, I present a few basics that will help make you a smart Hold'Em poker player in the actual casino environment, which is considerably different from any home game you may have played before.

Texas Hold'Em is similar to Seven-Card Stud poker only in that seven cards are dealt out in the end, and five of the seven cards are used by players to make the best possible hand they can make. But this is where the similarity ends. In Hold'Em all players at the table get two cards face down, which only they can see, but the remaining five cards are dealt face up, in front of the dealer, and are common cards to all the players in the game. This means that if these five common cards have among them, say, two kings, these two kings are common to everyone at the table who is still in the game at that point. All players can use these two kings to combine with the two cards they have, plus any of the remaining cards in the common cards dealt out.

How the Game Is Played

Texas Hold'Em tables are usually bigger than Seven-Card Stud tables, and can accommodate twelve players, and in some games even fourteen players. Generally, however, the tables will be limited to ten players. Most Hold'Em games start with the $1–$4 limit, but generally the majority of games are the $4–$8 variety. Other games offer the "$3-$6-$8 on the end" option, meaning that in the last round players can bet up to $8 and raise up to $8 (and some games even $12 on the end). Still other games offer $5–$10, $25–$50, and even $100–$200 limits, or higher for some games, but generally the game you are likely to encounter most often is the $4–$8 limit game. The best way to understand these limits is to learn that when the poker room announces or advertises their games, they will say something like, "Now spreading four-eight-eight Hold'Em." What this means is that they are starting a Texas Hold'Em game, and that the limits are a set amount of $4, and then $8 and then $8 (meaning that the initial round of betting before the flop is at the $4, on the flop at $4, on the turn at $8, and on the river at $8), and that these are "structured" amounts, meaning that any wager must be in at least those amounts, and all raises must be in those increments.

This is different from games that are shown as "from 1 to 4 and 4 to 8." This would mean that prior to the flop and on the flop the players could wager from $1 up to $4, but do not have to bet the full $4 on these rounds, as they would in the structured game I described above. Structured limits are usually shown as 4-8-8 for those limits. Nonstructured games are usually shown as 1-4-8-8 for those limits. Therefore, whenever you see any live poker game with limits posted with firm figures, such as 4-8-8, 3-6-12, or 10-20, you'll know that this is a *structured* game, and that all betting rounds must be made in those amounts, and those amounts only, and that all other rounds must be at those stated amounts, and all raises must be in those same increments. On the other hand, if you see a table limit posted as 1-4-8-8, 1-5-10, or whatever the amounts may be—if it says $1 at the beginning, this usually means that this is a *nonstructured* game, and that you can bet from $1 up to the stated limit amount for any round of betting. You do not have to make the maximum limit wager, as you would in all structured games. That's how you tell the games apart, and this is very important to know. Basically, the smaller Seven-Card Stud games, and many small limit Hold'Em games, will be in the nonstructured format, and will be shown as, for example, "from $1–$4" (and so on) for whatever the limits may be. Avoid nonstructured games, and confine your play only to structured games. This will potentially mean more profits for you, less cost in rake, and less "chasing" of hands, and consequently will also force you to play better. There are many more reasons why structured games are vastly better for you than nonstructured games, but we will leave that discussion for another time.

Texas Hold'Em uses a standard fifty-two-card deck, no jokers and no wild cards. As in all poker games, the cards are shuffled at the end of each game. The procedure is generally that which is known as shuffle, shuffle, box, shuffle, cut, and deal. The dealer then begins to deal clockwise. Which player gets the first card out depends on the position of the "dealer's puck," a small, white, round, plastic object that looks like a hockey puck. This is very similar to the one used in Craps, except in Hold'Em it has two white sides and each side has the word "dealer" written on it. This puck moves from player to player, clockwise, after each deal so that no single player will always get the first card out, thereby altering the sequence of hands that players get. Whoever holds the puck will get the *last* card of each turn of the deal. That's what makes this "puck" so important, because being the last to act in Hold'Em is a key ingredient in your playing skills and profitability. The player sitting to the left of the player with the dealer's puck gets the first card, player to his left the next card, and so on. The player on the left of the player holding the puck also has to make an ante blind bet of $1 (in a $3–$6 game—higher in bigger limit or no-limit games), and the player next to him, on his left, has to place a $3 blind ante bet. These amounts vary depending on the table limits. This blind bet is in place of an ante requirement from all players, such as the one in some Seven-Card Stud games. Since the puck moves from player to player around the table, eventually all players will have to make such blind bets. If you do not make this bet, or call yourself "out" of that hand, or leave the table while it is your turn, you get no cards, and now have to wait until the puck comes back around to you in order to be allowed to play again. You can, however, buy yourself back in the game at any time after you missed your blind bet turn by betting both blind bets out of turn (in most casinos, known as "making up the blinds" or "coming in between blinds").

This is done both because these players are in the first spot, getting the first and second cards out, but also to place some action on the table. If there is no action, and all players fold except one player, that player still gets a small win. These are usually called the "small blind" and the "big blind"—the small blind if the player immediately to the left of the button makes a blind bet usually about half the amount of the big blind. In a $3–$6 game, the small blind is usually $1 and the big blind $3. The player making the $3 big blind bet will also get a chance to raise after the first two cards have been dealt, and after all other players in the game have indicated either check, bet, or raise—called an "option"—provided, of course, there have been no other raises before the action returns to the player posting the big blind. The player making the small blind bet will be asked to call the big blind, or raise, provided there has been no other raise before the action returns to her. After the first set of cards is dealt out on the flop, the player in the small blind will also be the first player asked to check or bet.

In Hold'Em, all players get two cards face down, and these are the two cards that only they see. Betting takes place first after the initial two cards are dealt to each player. When all players have checked, bet, called, or folded, the flop takes place. The "flop" are three cards dealt face up by the dealer, who first burns one card, and then deals out the three that he turns over. These three cards turned are the flop, and are the first three of a total of five cards that will be dealt face up in front of the dealer. Betting takes place after the flop; then the dealer burns another card and deals one more card face up—called the "turn." More betting takes place, then the dealer burns another card and deals out the final fifth card—called the "river"—also face up. These five cards, face up—beginning with the flop and progressing two more rounds of one card per round until all five are seen—are common cards to all the players in the game. The object of Hold'Em is to use a combination of any of the five common cards with the two cards each player has to make the best possible five-card poker hand.

Let's say that you have an ace of clubs and a jack of diamonds as your two cards, face down, which only you can see. On the flop you may see ace of diamonds, 10 of diamonds, and 3 of clubs. Therefore, so far, you have two aces, and three-to-the-diamond flush. Let's say that the next card out is jack of clubs. Therefore you now have two pairs: two aces and two jacks. But you also have three to the flush in both diamonds and clubs. However, since there is only *one* more card to be dealt, whatever that card is you *cannot* make a Flush in *either* clubs or diamonds. Thus, the hand you are playing are the two pairs: the two aces and the two jacks, with the possible draw of either a jack or an ace on the final card to make you a full house. At this point you should remember that *all* the common cards can be used by *all* the other players still in the hand with you. Unlike in Seven-Card Stud, although you see the cards, you cannot make the same kind of judgments on the possible values of your opponents' hands. One of your opponents may have two clubs in hand, or two diamonds in hand, and therefore needs only either one to make a flush. In this case, if you don't get the full house, your two pair will be no good against a flush. It is for this reason that the betting and playing strategy in Hold'Em is vastly different from Seven-Card Stud.

How to Bet

Before we get into simple strategy, I will briefly outline the sequence of bets, using the $3–$6 game as the basis for the example. Let's say that you are not one of the players required to make the $1 or $3 blind bet at the beginning of the new deal. In this case you get the first two cards without having to make any bets—yet. After you get the first two cards (face down, which only you can see), the first round of betting occurs. If you think your two-card hand is good enough for you to take a chance on playing at least to the flop, which most players will do, you wait your turn and then bet accordingly. Each player, at each round of betting, can check, call, raise and check-and-raise, or fold. To "check" means you are making no bet. You can do this only if the players in front of you in the round of betting have made no bets. Since the players next to the dealer's puck have already bet $1 and $3 each, respectively, you cannot check on the opening round in Hold'Em. Your only option is to call, raise, or fold.

To "call" means you bet the same amount of money that was bet by the player ahead of you in the turn of betting. You do this by putting that amount of gaming chips in front of your position, and calling out "call." Don't throw your chips in the pot. This will confuse the dealer since your chips will scatter around the chips already in the pot and the amount you bet will not be clearly seen. This is called "splashing the pot" and is a bad thing to do. It can raise the ire of the other players, dealer, and floorman, and can even get you tossed out of the game if you continue to do it.

To "raise" means that you first place the amount of the "call" bet in front of you, while at the same time clearly calling out "raise," then placing the amount of your raise next to the "call" bet. You must call out "raise," or have the total amount of your bet in your hand clearly visible as being a raise. You should clearly call out the word "raise," as that will avoid a lot of confusion about your intentions. If you simply throw out the chips, chances are that the dealer will assume you are only calling the bet, and will not accept the raise. Often if you don't say out loud the word "raise," no amount of pleading will alter the fact that you failed to follow the rules. Other players at the table can get very angry at you for trying to make a "string bet." A string bet is when you don't call a raise and don't announce your intention, but are trying to "string" extra money in the pot. Because raising alters betting decisions for all other players, it is important that you clearly announce your decision to raise and then raise by the correct amount. You can, for example, call the $3 bet while at the same time calling out "raise $3," and place a total of $6 in front of you. This is a clear indication to everyone at the table that you raised the bet. They then have to match it, meaning "call" it, raise it again, or fold and get out of the hand.

To "check and raise," allowed in almost all major casino poker rooms, means you "check" your hand during the round of betting, and if a bet is made, or raised by another player and the turn comes back to you before the next card is dealt, you can raise again. This is a ploy exploited by smart players to raise the stakes of the pot, especially in circumstances where such a player has a good hand, usually the very best hand known as "the nuts." Check-and-raise options are good for strategy and can often build up a mediocre pot into a big one.

To "fold" simply means to discard your cards by throwing them, face down, to the dealer—and often also saying "fold." This means you are out of this hand and will take no action. You do this if you have garbage and don't want to risk your money on a bad hand with few possibilities. You then have to wait until the next hand to play again. If, however, you are the player who is required to make the $3 blind bet, don't fold if all players just call this first-action bet. If this happens, and you have a bad hand, throwing it away makes no sense since you have already bought your way into the flop round. Who knows . . . the flop may turn your garbage into the winning hand. I've seen this happen often enough. If, however, players at the table raise the bets, and it comes back to you and your hand looks like trash, fold and get out. Garbage in, garbage out—a good philosophy to follow.

If you are the player who made the big blind bet, and all other players simply call this action, you will be asked: "Option?" This means the dealer wants to know if you will exercise your option to raise the bets. If your hand is good, do it. Then all other players at the table have to either call, raise, check, or fold, and this goes around again until all players check or call or reraise. Only then will the next round begin, and so on.

After the flop another round of betting takes place, and the same principles of betting follow. Same for the turn and river—the final round. At the final round, when all still-active players have called the bets, the showdown takes place. Players still in the game turn over their two hole cards, and the dealer makes the best comparison between each player's set of two hole cards and the five common cards. Whichever player has the best five-card poker hand, using his two hole cards and any of the five common cards, is declared the winner. She gets the pot and all the money.

In almost all casino poker games there's a limit of three raises per round if more than two players are in the game. If there are only two players left betting, they can raise each other until doomsday, or until one of them is "all in," meaning he has no more active gaming chips on the table with which to bet. Eventually either this happens, or one of the players calls the other and we're back at the showdown. The best poker hand wins. With the exception of high-limit games, all games usually found in casino poker do not allow cash money to play. This means that if you have a $20 bill on the table, and are short of gaming chips for the bet you wish to make, you're plum out of luck. Money doesn't play, and so you will be called "all in" and, if there are still more rounds of betting to take place, a side pot will be made for those players who continue the action past your turn. This is the same procedure that takes place if you have used the last of your gaming chips on any bet in any round. The size of this side pot will depend on the action the table gets after you have been declared "all in." You are still in the game, but only in the initial pot, and not the side pot. The side pot winners are decided and paid first after the conclusion of all action on that hand. Then the main pot is decided, and your hand figures in this action. If your hand is the best, you still win the main pot.

"Betting out of turn" is not allowed. If players don't pay attention, or are tired, they can lose their place and bet out of turn. This is bad for them and bad for the other players. A bet out of turn indicates anxiety on the part of the culprit, or carelessness, and does that player only harm and never any good. It also tells the other players the state of mind of the guilty party, and often can alter the betting strategy of other players, particularly the players still in front in the turn of bets. Do yourself a big favor: If you're too tired, don't play. If you play, pay enough attention not to make silly mistakes like this.

Simple Strategy

In Hold'Em it is possible to win a pot with absolute garbage in hand. I said above that "garbage in, garbage out" is a good philosophy to follow, and I hold to that principle. However, a hand that looks great—potentially—with the first two cards can turn to garbage on the flop. How you play the hand then determines whether you win. For example, you may have an ace and a queen of spades as your two hole cards, a pretty good hand to stay in with to the flop, yet on the flop the three cards showing may fall as: 2 of clubs, 8 of diamonds, and 10 of hearts. Garbage. There is nothing you can do with this hand unless you pull an ace or a queen in the next two cards, still to come, to make a pair. Maybe even two pairs if you're very lucky. This is called having "over-cards," but, practically speaking, this hand is trash. However, you have a high hand, relative to the flop. If, for example, no other cards come out that make any pair or any hand for any player at the table, your ace-queen is quite likely to be the winner. In essence, your garbage is better than someone else's garbage. The only hand that can beat you is an ace-king combination (or any pair). In this example, you should be able to tell whether other players have better hands than you by the way they bet. Of course they may be trying to "buy" the pot, meaning they have nothing but bet aggressively to give the other players the impression they have something, knowing that the flop shows garbage. Most of the time this ploy works if indeed other players have garbage and simply decide it's not worth the risk of spending more money on the off chance the aggressive bettor is actually bluffing. Also, in some circumstances, if, say, you and another player hammer this out to the end, and both of you have an ace-queen, the hand will be a tie and the pot split between you.

Sometimes, however, there may be an open pair on board, meaning that the winning hand is common to all players. This is called "playing the board," meaning that your two hole cards do not figure in the best possible poker hand combination. If this happens, and you have the ace-queen, and your one other opponent has, say, queen-jack, your ace will play and you win. Again, the rules of poker apply, and the best possible hand wins, even if this winning hand simply constitutes that lone ace that makes your garbage better than the garbage played by your opponents. As you can see, there is a whole lot more to Hold'Em than first meets the eye. The simple basics will help you get into the game, but you should observe the game first, and ask the dealers and players and supervisors to help you as well. Most of the time, especially in the smaller games in small casinos, there will be enough time, and enough staff and players, to help you understand the game better. Don't be afraid to take what you have learned here and improve your knowledge and skills by actually trying it out in the casinos. Such experience is priceless. Your skills can only develop by actually playing the real game in the real casino.

Hold'Em is a tough game because of the many possibilities embodied in the use of five common cards, seen by all players in the game to that point, combined with the two hole cards held by each player in the game. Observation of the cards, as in Seven-Card Stud, will not help nearly as much, although learning to spot trends in how other people play will help. Here are a few hints as introduction to simple strategy:

- Although in Seven-Card Stud it is a good idea to play your opponent's hand to lose, in Hold'Em it is important to play your hand to win.
- In Hold'Em, whether you win with your good hand, a marginal hand, or even a bad hand depends directly on how you bet and when you bet.
- Stay in the game to see the flop if you have at least a king-queen, off-suit, ace-anything suited, ace-10 or higher off-suit, or at least queen-jack, suited.
- If you stay in the opening round, before the flop, call the bets made and raise only if other players have bet or called without hesitation. If they raise more than once, and you have no pocket pair or ace in the hole, fold before it costs you more money.
- If you have a pocket pair, call if it's a low pair (that is, 2s through 9s); raise if you have a pocket pair of 10s, jacks, or queens; raise and reraise, if possible, if you have a pocket pair of kings or aces.
- After the flop, if you improve your hand marginally, and it is not your turn to open the betting, see how the other players bet. If they bet aggressively, and several raises take place before it is your turn, call the bets. If no one raises, then you raise. If you are reraised, call. If it's your turn to open the betting, check and see what happens. If you are called, and not raised, check and raise. If you are raised, call. If you have a great

hand after the flop—three-of-a-kind, two high pair, or even better—bet the maximum allowed for that round and see what happens. Chances are you will get called. If you are raised, call and don't reraise. At this point, with a great hand, you don't want to overplay the hand and get other players to drop out before you can get more of their money into the pot.

- On the turn, if your hand has improved, or you still have the good hand you started with, and nothing else shows up that could potentially beat your hand, bet your hand to the hilt. Now is the time to get other players out of the game. If other players are fishing, your hard action will tell them to watch out, and chances are they will fold and thus not place you in danger of losing your good hand if they get lucky on the last card. However, if some other player bets into you aggressively, chances are that player also has a good hand, maybe a better hand than you. In that case raise him two times, and if he raises again, call him.

- When the final seventh card is dealt on the river, and it's your turn to open the betting, bet as aggressively as you did on the turn, regardless of what the last card meant to your hand. If it's not your turn to open the betting, wait to see what other players will do. If other players still in the game bet aggressively and raise before it's your turn, raise again, but only call the next raise if the bet is raised yet again. If other players simply bet and call, and it comes your turn, raise. If called, chances are you have the winning hand. If raised again, call, but look at the flop and see what possibilities there may be for such a player. If you're pretty sure you still have the winning hand, calling this bet is better than raising again only to find out the other player did pick up a winner on the last card. At this point the amount of your call-bet is small relative to the amount you already invested in the pot, so such a call is worth the risk even if you are marginally unsure of the other player's hand. But be warned that raising the bet in this circumstance could result in your being caught in the "war of raises," and, should that other player actually beat you, cost you too much money relative to your pot investment up to that point.

- Fold your hand at the opening round if you don't have at least a king-queen off-suit, ace-anything suited, ace-10 or higher off-suit, or at least queen-jack, suited. After the flop, fold your hand if you don't improve it, or if the action by other players is heavy. Fold your hand on the turn only if other players bet too big relative to your pot investment so far, and your hand is merely marginal. Always fold your hand anytime if you're not sure it can win, especially if other players at the table bet vigorously. Chances are your hunch is right, and you would have merely fed the pot.

- Don't bluff too much. Though bluffing is an integral part of winning in Hold'Em, especially when you are in the last position or second-to-last (which is a distinct advantage, unlike Seven-Card Stud), bluffing in Hold'Em can cost you a lot. There are simply too many possibilities for other players to make winners over your garbage if you're bluffing. I've seen players bluff only to be called on the bluff by a good player and beat with a lowly pair of deuces, or even just ace high. You will need to be a pretty good player of Hold'Em before you can make a stone-cold bluff stand up.

- Just as important as not overplaying your good hand is not underplaying a bad hand. A bad hand may look marginal at the opening round, maybe even after the flop, yet quickly become better on the turn. Sometimes, especially in the opening round before the flop, if the action is heavy, you can build yourself a pot by overplaying a hand that normally you wouldn't bet so big. Usually if this happens, other players at the table also have marginal hands and, as in the ace-queen example above, you can get yourself a winner by making them all think you're the power at the table. But don't do this too often, because this is a borderline bluff. If you're lucky on the draw, you may wind up looking as good as you were betting, but if you're not so lucky, you can easily get called and caught. Once caught bluffing, or overplaying a marginal hand, your odds of winning on sloppy hands go down the drain.

More Thoughts on Hold'Em, Poker, and Gambling in General

I'm certain that by now you get the idea of how complex casino poker can be. Playing poker at home, with friends, allows for flexibility that casino poker simply does not have. In casino live poker, chances are that at least one of the people at your table will be a professional. Sometimes there are two pros at the table, playing in teams. If you approach casino poker with the hometown poker player attitude you'll get cleaned out quickly. Casino live poker is a great game to enjoy, but be wary of what you're getting into. Poker is a game of many skills. Playing it by luck alone will quickly make you a loser, but if you play smart, you soon grasp the basics of what your choices are, when to apply them, and why you are making them. This approach will provide you with a rewarding poker experience with at least the knowledge that you can hold your own. Here's a small piece of advice: Don't get distracted by the casino environment, the noise, hustle, cocktail servers, talk at the table, or antics by some players. Play your cards, be cool, don't drink, and watch other players and how they play.

There are a whole slew of situations that you will encounter, in Texas Hold'Em, in casino poker, and among many casino games. It is important that you learn the odds and percentages, and look to the mathematics of gambling as a useful guide; however, overreliance on such information is not the answer. Casino gaming, and life in general, is not composed merely of numbers to quantify and exponentiate. Life, and casino gaming, is endowed with a plethora of variables, none of which can fit into the neat confines of the mathematical, puritanical "box" of so-called truths. For example, when nuclear physicists first discovered the occurrence of neutrinos, they were able to postulate the existence of neutrinos theoretically but weren't able to actually see them until the advent of the particle accelerators that provided for the possibility of smashing atoms, thereby releasing a multitude of particles that could then be seen as actual physical representations. Until then the mathematical theory of particle physics predicted that the neutrinos would act in a predictable manner, and disperse in accordance with a certain dispersion curvature. Unfortunately, when the particles were actually observed, they acted in a manner that was anything but in accordance with the theory of dispersion. In fact, they acted completely randomly, with absolutely no discernible pattern. Each and every test thereafter produced a completely new and unpredictable pattern of dispersion—so much so that for the first time physicists actually began to admit the possibility that the theory of chaos might actually have some validity.

The point is that in gambling the dispersion patterns of events aren't always perfect and don't always follow the presupposed theory. There is more to gaming success than just the numbers, though many gaming experts are prone to overusing mathematical percentages, frequencies of occurrence, and probabilities, and in general overusing the importance of mathematics in gambling. Mathematics is a useful tool. Without mathematics, gambling would not be possible, at least not the way we understand it now in the world of casinos and casino games. For example, if we have a starting hand of two aces and a suited 10 in Seven-Card Stud, we may know that the mathematics indicates that we will make a straight flush about 0.02 percent of the time, or that we will make three of a kind about 9.75 percent of the time, or that we will make two pairs about 41 percent of the time. Simple math, right?

Well, not entirely. Although such a sequence of cards will, inevitably, prove to be so in the long run of infinite statistical probability doesn't mean that it will do so for you while you are actually playing. Computer programs that are written for tests such as these which produce the overall statistics for poker hands, based on the randomness of expected probability, aren't perfect. Perfection, as a concept, is all but impractical in the real world, and not just in gambling. Your home computer isn't perfect, and neither is mathematics as a science. In mathematics, there are no absolutes. The truisms expressed in mathematical terms are in themselves based on certain assumptions, many of which are totally unsupported by any empirically derived circumstances. In fact truisms are largely vacuous in concept. They may have absolute inherent values within their own designated parameters, but they are for all intents and purposes useless. An algebraic truism such as $(a = a)$ may be absolute, but useless for anything but itself. And mathematical equations such as $1 + 1 = 2$ may be useful in determining values, but they are based on assumptions of perceived reality of whole numbers, and their meaning within specified circumstances. So what does all this mean for poker players, or gamblers in general?

It means that the expected probability of making a hand, or of a win or loss, is an assumption, one based in large part on a further set of assumptions that went into the creation of the mathematical profile of that hand's statistical probability ranking and odds. In addition, such series of mathematical assumptions are further compromised, versus the real world of in-casino play, by the fact of the testing and research that goes into the validation of such hand's ranking and percentage of event calculations. These tests involve a whole series of probability tests, vested in the principles of probability calculus and event actuality. Such tests are conducted under laboratory conditions and consist of millions of simulations done with computers. These computer tests themselves run on other computer programs, and in the end they provide an analysis of the relative frequencies of occurrences that are then computed to equate to the expected percentages. This then becomes the basis for the probability ranking of such hands under the designated starting and ending circumstances.

What is missing in all of this is the reality of the short-term play by players in the actual casino. No poker player will play the game for the same number of consecutive events that were part of the tests for that sequence of hands. Machines are used to perform these tests and calculations. Consequently, what are missing in all such mathematically derived recommendations for profitable play, whether for poker hands or any other gambling game, are the facts of the limited exposure by the player to that sequence of hands, or game.

Of course it is better to play a hand whose starting percentage value is statistically higher than another. That is simple common sense. However, reliance on such numbers alone isn't. If you continually choose to play hands simply and only based on the expected mathematical probability of event occurrences, you will lose more often than not. In your actual in-casino play, you will play any given hand at far less than the overall mathematically derived probabilities of event occurrence. No matter what starting hand you select, even the better-odds higher rank hands, your individual event-occurrence expectation will not be anything close to the overall mathematics of that hand's overall percentages. You will either win the pot at a rate far higher than the mathematical probabilities indicate, or far less. You will either win a lot more than the mathematics indicate, or not nearly as much. Therefore, the reality is that *choosing any poker hand solely based on the averages of expected event probability of occurrence* won't do. Overreliance on mathematics as a guide for gambling success is inherently flawed.

Your choices of hands to play need be far more "variable." And variables are the death knell for mathematicians. Mathematics does not like variables, because by their very nature they are mathematically indefinable. What this means is that anything that cannot be expressed in whole-number absolutes, even allowing for fractions, is untenable (and indefinable). As a direct result, your success in gambling, and in poker, is not wholly dependent on such numerical factors alone. The variables in your choices of hands are factors such as your:

- Play observation
- Action given to that table
- Play time and bankroll
- Betting strategy
- Psychological predisposition to attractiveness of certain kinds (such as "liking" certain hands, draws, opponents, and pot odds)
- Aptitude
- Skills
- Ability to notice and adapt
- Resiliency
- Dedication to abstinence from depressants such as alcohol while gambling

There are dozens more reasons and situations of this kind, all mathematically indefinable variables, all of which contribute to your overall gambling success.

Gaming experts have overemphasized mathematics as the end-all holy grail of gambling success—and I include myself in this group in some of my earlier writings. It is easy to see why. Numbers and percentages are easy to see, view, understand, and explain. They are the ideal "tool" by which to try to impart knowledge to readers—a *tool* for *explanations,* but *not* the sum total of all successes in gambling.

This is not a problem confined to gambling. We are human creatures in a desperate search for order. We expect order wherever we look, and if we don't find it, we find ways of creating it. It helps us understand. But before you embark on a study of the mathematics of gambling you need to make one basic decision:

Are you playing for entertainment? or are you playing for profit?

If your answer is *entertainment,* then your reliance on mathematically derived assistance is a waste of time. You should instead rely on assistance derived from the variables, as listed above.

If your answer is *profit,* then you need to combine the realistic differential between cold mathematics and the real world of your exposure to that set of circumstances, combined further with your particular selection of variables. This combination will constitute your individual success rate.

The mathematics of gambling as I have chosen to apply it and describe it here applies equally to your choices of any gambling game. While much has been written about the "odds" and "percentages" inherent in gambling games (and table games in particular), the fact is that the limited exposure any gambler will have to these games all but eliminates any odds-advantages in such mathematically perfect play, versus the inherent disadvantages in the game's rules, thus completely disallowing and forgetting even one of the most important game factors—the game's volatility index. The sad reality is that some players will win even when playing extremely badly and making the kinds of decisions on which gaming purists frown, including playing decisions that are horrendously wrong.

Your decisions about what game to play, and how to play it, should not be solely vested in principles of mathematics. Just because a decision in poker, for example, calls for—let's say—a reraise, as based on the mathematically derived sets of rules for pot odds and expected probability of a win based on the hand value, doesn't mean that at that precise instant you should always do so. There may be other variables to factor in this decision. In the real world, where nothing is fixed, your decision to ignore the math and probabilities may bring you far more profit.

Overreliance on mathematics, odds information, and probability calculus can lead one to expect events that simply will not occur for that slice of the overall reality you will experience as a player at that game, and with those hands. Your personal adaptability to these situations is the key factor to continued success. Your successes, or failures, in gambling have far more to do with *your ability to adapt to the circumstances at hand,* and far less to do with the odds or percentages of expected events, or overall mathematical statistics. Poker players can make a living at poker because they have learned how, and when, to disregard the mathematics. The same applies to the few professional blackjack players who can affect the overall outcome of their sessions, as well as to any other player who desires to play professionally or has at least mastered the principles of game variance.

Adapting is not as hard as it may seem. Yes, you should learn all that you can about the game, its odds, percentages, and overall mathematics, but then put it away in the back of your mind. Play the games based on actual event experiences, and learn to modify your decisions in an instant. Take into account all the variables of the experience and the psychological factors, including your own mood at the moment, and adapt your decisions accordingly. And that's how you will be able to keep yourself ahead, more than behind, in your gaming success.

Live Poker—Seven-Card Stud

Seven-Card Stud is by far the most popular game among casino poker patrons (along with Texas Hold 'Em), perhaps because it closely resembles the poker games most of us have played at home. The generally lower betting limits also make the game attractive to casual players. In most casinos, betting limits for Seven-Card Stud begin with "$1–$4" as the lowest limits available, no ante. This means that on any round of betting you can bet as low as $1, or as much as $4, but no less and no more. You can also raise by this same range of amounts. Often the pot grows when there are several raises. If one player raises $2, for example, and your turn comes next and you wish to raise, you can call the $2 and raise $4, for a total of $6. That's how even small-limit games, like $1–$4, can produce some very decent pots. There is also a game called "$1–$4–$8 on the end." This is the same $1–$4 game but with the added option of betting up to $8 in the final round, after the seventh card has been dealt. At this point all players still in the game know what their final hands are and, presumably, all have what they consider good hands. It is therefore an advantage for players to have the option of betting larger amounts, especially when they think, or know, they have the winning hand. This round is called the "showdown." Seven-Card Stud games offer a variety of betting limits, from the $1–$4 and the eight-on-the-end option, to $5–$10, $10–$20, $20–$30, and $50–$100 as the most common games seen in poker rooms. Other higher-betting-limit games are also in progress, but very rarely will such a game actually take place in the main casino poker room. Those high-stakes games are usually played in the private rooms provided by casinos for their high-rolling clientele.

INTRODUCTION TO SEVEN-CARD STUD

How the Game Begins

Since there is usually no ante required, the dealer begins by dealing two cards face down and one card face up to each of the players at the table. Eventually the player whose first up card is the lowest in face value of all cards showing has to open the betting. Dealing is done clockwise, and each player gets one card until all players have one card, then the second card until all players have two cards, and finally the third card face up until all players have a third card. This is the first round. The "ante" is an opening blind bet—prior to dealing—which is used in some games. Basically this is an investment in the game and an indication that the player is in this hand. It is often used to increase the value of the pot from the get-go. Often in poker games, especially in low-limit Seven-Card Stud games, antes are used to make a game of it. It is not unusual to see almost all the players fold their hands even before the next round begins, and the winner would therefore not win anything. Using the ante in these circumstances provides the winner with at least some kind of a win. In most games there is also the "bring in." This is a forced bet, usually the smallest amount available in the betting structure, such as $1 in the most popular small-limit games. The player who receives the lowest-value card on the initial deal, by number value and suit, is forced to start the betting with the bring-in. That forced bet is in addition to the antes, should the game also have antes. All poker rooms that play Seven-Card Stud in the casinos will have a forced bring-in, although many won't have an ante. It all depends. Games with an ante and a bring-in are a little more expensive to play, but are generally better because there's more win potential.

In Seven-Card Stud, seven cards in total will eventually be dealt out. The first two are face down for all players; only you get to see the first two cards dealt to you. Then, in turn, four cards will be dealt face up to each player, one for each round of betting. Finally, in the last round, the seventh card is dealt face down to each player. Therefore, if you stay in the game, you will have three cards face down (which only you can see) and four cards face up, which your opponents can see as well. You, of course, can also see your opponents' cards. The object of the game is to use your seven cards to make the best five-card poker hand. This provides for many possibilities. Some players may be showing a possible strong hand in the four cards face up, but have nothing in the three cards face down. This allows for a good portion of "bluffing" in Seven-Card Stud. At other times the four cards showing may look like garbage, but when combined with the three cards only that player sees eventually make a great hand.

Success in Seven-Card Stud, and in poker generally, directly depends on skill level. Knowledge of the game, betting strategies, observation of other players (how they bet and their personal habits)—all are an indication of how successful you can be. Yes, luck of the draw also plays an important part, but how you conduct your betting strategy for each round of bets, and how well you know the cards and the possible winning combinations for your set of cards, all contribute to winning. Since you see four of your opponents' seven cards, you can make judgments on what possible hands they have. Of course they do the same to you. In addition, if you keep track of what cards are out, you can also make adequate judgments on the likelihood that your hand will improve with each successive round, all the way to the final, seventh, card.

Simple Strategy

A standard fifty-two-card deck is used, no jokers, and there are no wild cards in Seven-Card Stud. Because Seven-Card Stud offers you the opportunity to see the seven cards you have, plus four of the seven each of your opponents has (all those players who have stayed with you at least till the sixth card) it is not too difficult to calculate which cards are still left. This makes most sense when applied to the probability of you improving a hand with a good draw. But you don't see all the cards. If the table is full, seven to nine players total, not all players will stay in the game. Most will stay to see the fourth card out, fewer will stay for the fifth card, and even fewer for the sixth card. Of those who stayed till 6th street, as the sixth card round is often called, chances are that most will stay in to see the final card. These players already have a good hand, or can improve on a good hand, or can have a great hand with a one-card draw: the final card. Of course there is always the possibility that a player will stay in the hand till the end, bet aggressively, and be bluffing. Sometimes you can spot such a bluff, and if you do you can usually outbluff the bluffer.

The people waiting to make a hand on the final card, without already having a good hand, are called "fishermen," because they are "fishing" for the one card that will make them a good hand. If they catch it, it is often called "caught on the river." This terminology has a historical base in the old riverboat gamblers of the nineteenth century.

Whether the remaining players on 6th street will stay in the hand for the final card also depends on the round of betting. If there are four players left, and two bet aggressively, chances are that at least one of the other two will fold, not wishing to spend more money for a fishing trip. But such aggressive players may also be bluffing, so it is important for you to know how to bet and how to apply your personal strategy to poker play. Because of such player attrition, you will never see all the cards dealt face up, or those that would have been dealt face up had all players stayed in the game. Therefore, depending on the cards you do get to see, it is important that you make relative judgments on which of the cards that *you may possibly get* could improve your hand. Also, after each turn, each new card dealt, the dealer also burns a card in between rounds. This is another card you don't see, and it is done to avoid sequential dealing or the possibility of cheating. On the average, in Seven-Card Stud you will see slightly less than half the cards in the fifty-two-card deck. Sometimes more, and sometimes fewer, depending on the number of players at the table and how many of them stay in the hand until 6th street.

If, for example, you have two pair going into the seventh, and final round, and you need one more of either card to make a full house, chances of drawing such a card depend directly on which cards have already been dealt out. If you are holding, for example, two kings and two jacks, you need either one more king or one more jack to make the full house. If you've been observant, you have noticed that throughout the six rounds two kings have been dealt out.

This means all four kings are out: you're holding two, and you saw the other two dealt out. Therefore there is no chance that you can get another king. You are now reduced to fishing for the jack. But what if you also saw another jack dealt out? That means there is only one card left in the deck that can improve your hand. Of course, you may not have seen these cards dealt out. Another player still in the game can be holding the pocket pair of kings, like you, and perhaps another holds a pocket pair of jacks. In either case, how you proceed with your game depends on what you consider the value of your two pairs to be. Kings and jacks is not a bad hand. If, in evaluating the possible hands other players in the game may have, you think that those two high pairs are enough, stay in till the final round. Chances are that you will win with the high two pairs, or may even get that extra card for an even better hand. But you should be playing the cards you *have,* and not the cards you *hope* to have. Other players may already have a hand, and, as in fishing, sometimes you catch the big one—but more often than not you wind up losing your bait.

If, for example, you have this high two-pair hand, and you see another player with three- or even four-to-a-flush, chances are that she does have the flush. Therefore your only chance of winning is to draw to that full house. If you do, you have a live one and can bet aggressively and win a lot from the player with the flush. But if you have already seen all but one of the cards out that could make you a full house, fold. It hurts to fold such a high two-pair hand, especially if, after the hand is over, you see that the player really didn't have the flush, but only a small pair, and still won because you threw your hand in. Folding like this is still smart play. You didn't take a crazy chance, you observed the cards and the play, and you played and bet accordingly. Over a session in this poker game, *smart* play will make you a winner more often than *crazy* play. Also, luck of the draw can be your best friend—or your bitter enemy. If you're on the receiving end of a favorable flow of cards, it seems like you can do no wrong. But even if this happens, don't be surprised if you don't win much. It's quite likely that other players at the table will spot the good hands you are getting early in the rounds and simply not stay in with you. How you bet in these cases will either make you a big winner or a small winner. The dilemma is if you bet aggressively early, you may get other players out and win only a little. But, if you bet conservatively, not showing the strength of your hand by the bets you make, you could let someone in. This means that a player with a mediocre hand, who would likely have folded had you bet aggressively, will stay in for the hell of it, and wind up drawing a better hand than yours. To resolve this dilemma, my mantra is: No win is a small win.

Any time you are a winner you have made money. If you're not positive you can beat any fisherman, bet to get them out of the game. This is especially important if you've had a run of the cards and won several hands, and players are now scared of you. Now is the time for you to bluff, especially if you are showing a halfway decent hand (which you know but they don't). It is almost a certainty that after such a streak other players will not risk money on even good hands against you, thinking that you, again, have a great hand. Bluffing like this is easier in Seven-Card Stud than in Hold'Em. In Seven-Card Stud your four cards may be showing such a strong hand that other players simply won't risk staying in with you, especially if you are betting as if you really have that hand. If you do, this will only reinforce this fear, and thereafter other players will be less likely to call your bluff. If you don't overdo this strategy you can bluff more often and win more often. If, however, you get called on the bluff, and lose, don't try it again until you reestablish the strength of your hands and your betting skills. Once you are seen as a bluffer, other smart players will bet into you and you can quickly lose any winnings you made up to that point.

Don't overdo it. If you bet big consistently, and win big consistently, other players at the table will either leave or simply not stay in the hands you are in until cards turn against you, or you make a silly mistake. Making any kind of consistent bets is a tell-tale sign of a novice player. Always vary your bets—when you bet, how much, how much you raise, and when. This way other players will not be able to tell what you have. Also watch your habits. Many players display the same behavioral tendencies when having either good hands, bad hands, or mediocre hands. Regular poker players will quickly be able to tell what you have even before you realize it. Often these tidbits of information are infinitesimal, and the person who does them is unaware. These "signs"—known as "tells"—can be as simple as playing with your gaming chips when you feel good because you see you have a good hand or scratching your nose when you know you have a bad hand, or a mediocre hand. Be aware of what you're doing—and revealing—and when, and then try to vary or reverse such behavior. This can work in your favor, because other players watching you will now think you have something other than what you do in fact have.

Don't be afraid to bet. Often people new to the game, or new to the casino environment of the game, underplay their hands. Underplaying good hands, or even marginal hands with good potential, will only result in some other player drawing a better hand. That player might not have stayed in the hand with you had you bet properly. To determine the possible value of your hand, just reread what you have read so far and apply the principles of observation and knowledge. If you are not certain about the quality of your hand, chances are your first impression was correct and the hand isn't worth playing. Fold it, and play another hand. Only staying in the hand will cost you money, and even if there is an ante at your Seven-Card Stud game, losing the half-dollar, or dollar, ante is better than playing a hand that can result in a greater loss. At the same time, if you do decide to stay in the hand, bet it for all it's worth. If you sit at your table with $100, consider that money gone. This is your stake, this is your loss limit. It no longer exists for you. It has become a tool. So use that tool and make it work. Betting "safe" in poker is a prescription for disaster. Scared money will fly away quickly. If you see your tendency going this way, take a break, or leave and play later. This also applies if you are not getting any cards to play. However, betting safe is different from betting conservatively. Betting safe means you underplay a good hand. Betting conservatively means you don't overplay a marginal hand and you never play a bad hand.

My final piece of advice is: Don't play your hand as a potential winner . . . play your *opponents'* hands as a *potential loser.* If you play your cards as a potential winner, and there are three other people still in the game with you, odds are 3:1 [against you] that one of these three other players has a hand better than yours. If you play your hand only as a potential winner, you're playing poker like an ostrich: you stick your head in the sand and hope the danger will go away. In all gambling games, but in poker especially, until the hand is over and the winner is decided, there's always a possibility that what you think of as a winning hand will wind up second best, or worse, third best. Time and again I have seen players feel confident in their hand, yet lose in the final round because they played their hand to win, rather than their opponents' hands to lose. This again comes down to your poker acumen, knowledge of the game, and betting strategy, and how well you keep track of your opponents' possible hands. Playing your opponents' hands to lose, rather than your hand to win, means that you shift the focus of your attention from feeling comfortable about *your* hand's possibilities, to anticipating the possible failures in your opponents' hands. If you have a good hand in poker, and have possibilities for improving it still, you already know what you have and what you need to make it better. Therefore, your hand should command little or no attention from now on. Your hand and its possibilities for improvement are a fact you have already calculated and are aware of, while your opponents' hands are not. Focus on those players who are still in the game with you. Make a quick calculation of what their apparent hands, and likely improvements, may be.

These decisions come into play in Seven-Card Stud mostly on 5th street and 6th street. The crucial point is the fifth card out. By this time it is possible for any player still in the game to already possess a great hand. After all, only five of the seven cards can be used to make a winning hand, and because Seven-Card Stud offers you the chance of seeing three of the first five cards, you can make fairly accurate judgments of hand potential if you look and pay attention to what you are seeing. While other players are busy making judgments about what hand you may possibly have, you already know. Therefore, devote your energy and powers of observation to what your opponents have, or what they can make out of what they have. This constitutes smart play in poker, because *your hand is only as good as your opponent's hand is bad.* Your hand may be four aces, but if your opponent draws a straight flush, your hand isn't worth a plugged nickel. In this example if you played your four aces to the hilt, and didn't bother to see the straight flush draw one of your opponents had, you'd be broke in one hand. Therefore, remember: Don't play your hand to win, play your opponent's hand to lose.

This simple strategy is possible in Seven-Card Stud, but in Texas Hold'Em the situation is quite different. In Texas Hold'Em it is not as easy to put your opponent on a hand, much less on a hand that is worse than yours. This is due not only to the fact that you don't see any of your opponent's possible cards, such as the four up cards you get to see in Seven-Card Stud, but also because most of the time you can't make any judgments as to the possibility of what your opponent's two down cards may be. In Seven-Card Stud, for example, if your opponent pairs his door card (his first up card) you know that this can be a sign of danger. Any time your opponent pairs his door card in this game, it can mean already a three of a kind, two pair, or possibly even four of a kind. It is a danger sign, and if you know how to read and react to it, and how to read and react to the player's actions based on that card on 4th street (the one that pairs the door card), then you can make pretty certain assumptions about the potential strength of that player's hand. In Hold'Em, however, you can't see your opponent's door card, because there isn't one. All you can do is assume the potential value of your opponent's two-down-card hand by what he does both before and after the flop. You can often also get additional such information after the turn, but by that time you should be pretty sure of what your opponent can have (or what *they* can have if there is more than one).

There is also the problem of "kickers," the cards whose value determines the final winning value of the five card final hand at showdown. For example, if you have an ace and a jack, and the flop is ace-4-7 in mixed suits, you now have a pair of aces, with your jack being your kicker. The kicker will come into play later, depending on what the other cards are on the turn and the river. Assuming that nothing else happens to counterfeit your hand on the turn and the river, let's see what happens if two other players also have an ace and are there with you at showdown. You have an ace and a jack, for a pair of aces. Let's say the board shows the five cards as follows: ace-4-7-9-2, in mixed suits. Both your opponents also have an ace in this example. The first player shows an ace and a 10. The second shows an ace and an 8. Your hand wins because your kicker is higher than theirs. The first player would make the following five-card hand from the seven cards on the game: her ace and 10, plus the ace on the board for the pair of aces, plus the two highest cards on the board, which are the 7 and the 9. So, this player's final five-card poker hand is ace-ace-7-9-10. She has a pair of aces, with the 7 and the 9 not being in effect, and her 10 is her kicker. The second player has a hand of ace-ace-7-9-8, with his 8 being his kicker. Your hand, however, shows the hand of ace-ace-7-9-jack. Your five-card poker hand is higher in value, because your jack plays, and it is the highest kicker. That is why kicker cards are so important in Texas Hold'Em. In that game many pots are won with only one pair, and the second player's card being the kicker often decodes who wins and who loses.

For these reasons, it is doubly important to play your hand for the value it has, the value it can have, and the value of your kicker card in the event that the showdown consists of the same pair as you have, as in the above example. The old saying among Hold'Em players is "Never leave home without a kicker." Trust this saying—believe me, it will come to mean a whole lot to you when you start playing Texas Hold'Em. Because of these vast differences between strategies and skills for Hold'Em and Seven-Card Stud, in Seven-Card Stud you can easily play your opponent's hand to lose, while in Hold'Em you should always play your hand to win. Always be on the lookout for any other player's potential higher hand, or higher-hand draw.

The best example I can give you is as follows: Let's say you have that ace and a jack to start with, and they are suited in hearts. On the flop, you hit ace-jack-4, with two of those cards—the ace and the jack—being suited in spades, and the 4 in diamonds. So, now you flopped what is usually a very good hand—the two highest pairs—but you have no hearts. Now say that on the turn comes the 8 of spades. Now there are three spades on the board. Another player comes out betting. What do you do? Well, this is a situation almost exactly like the one in Seven-Card Stud wherein your opponent pairs his door card. In Texas Hold'Em, something like this usually indicates that the betting player has made a flush. Your two pairs are no good if that is indeed the case. Unless you catch either an ace or a jack to make a full house, your hand is all but dead at this point, although it may be worth the call, depending on the player and the circumstances. Players who are bluffing often make a strong play on exactly this kind of a flop and turn, just to see if they can run over the pot and win by making other players throw away their better hands. You may wish to call, therefore, depending on the player who did the betting and your knowledge of how she plays. But what about this: The 10 of spades shows up on the river. You know there are four spades on the board, and three to the straight, plus three to the royal flush. Oh boy are you in trouble! So what now? What if the other player still comes out firing? Well, here's when your knowledge of your opponents, and how they play, and your knowledge of the game will bear the most fruit. At best, all you have is two pairs. Your opponent could easily have a flush, now needing only one spade among her two cards, while you don't have any spades and will lose this pot to any hand that does. Or, your opponent could have a straight, in which case you also lose. Or, worse still, she could have made a royal flush, in which case you are so much dog meat you shouldn't even think about playing that hand. Well, you see, it all depends on the players and your abilities to know what they do or don't have, and how they are likely to play it.

What if there are other players also still in this hand? What if one of them calls, and the other raises? Well, by now it should be obvious that if you don't have a spade, and a high one at that, and don't have a straight, your odds of winning are practically zero. Throw away the hand. The old saying among poker players in situations like this is: If one bets, he may have it or he may not. But if two others call or raise, one of them probably does. Remember this as well: If you don't have it, and you are in a multi-way pot with someone else doing the betting and others doing the calling, or raising, you are probably not the winner. Save money, and throw your hand in. Even if you later see that you would have won, the money you saved this time will be better spent on the next hand, plus you now have valuable information about what these other players do, and how they do it. This applies to all poker games, not just Hold'Em or Seven-Card Stud.

It all depends—and depends mostly on you.

Progressive Caribbean Stud

Caribbean Stud is a combination of poker and a slot machine. It is played on a blackjack-style table and features a five-card poker game similar to draw poker, but *no* draw, with an added $1 slot. Into this slot the players deposit a $1 gaming chip prior to the start of each hand, and it is this $1 that plays for the progressive jackpot plus offers bonus pays on hands of flush or better. This game is not new. Many players are familiar with it from cruise ships and Caribbean resorts. The innovation, however, is the progressive jackpot. It is offered in most Las Vegas casinos and in some other gaming jurisdictions.

INTRODUCTION TO PROGRESSIVE CARIBBEAN STUD

As with all casino games, you begin by changing your cash into gaming chips. Depending on how much money you offer to change, dealers will almost always break your chips into the most common denominations. For example, if you offer up $100, you will most likely get $90 in red $5 chips, and $10 in white $1 chips. Whatever the breakdown is, it doesn't matter to the game. You can request chips of any denomination, as long as this matches the table playing rules and limits. The game has a specific layout for betting, and traditionally has seven player positions. In front of each player position is a betting area, which has three distinct features: the ante bet, the bet box, and the progressive jackpot and bonus pay.

The Ante Bet

The "ante" is a *mandatory* required bet. If you do not make this bet, you cannot be in the next hand. The amount of this bet is determined by the table minimum limits set by the casino where you are playing. Most casinos will have a $5 minimum table bet limit; hence, the mandatory ante bet is $5. Other casinos may have different table limits. In Las Vegas, several casinos offer a $3 minimum, while most of the Strip casinos will have either $5 or $10 minimum ante bet requirements. The amount of this ante bet has no bearing on whether or not you will win. It does, however, have a bearing on *how much* you can win and how much you can lose, as well as how much of a bankroll you will require in order to play this game to your best advantage.

The Bet Box

Behind the mandatory ante bet area is a circular (or semi-circular) area marked as "bet." Once your cards have been dealt to you, *if* you wish to proceed with the game, you *must* bet *twice* the amount of your ante bet in this area. Once you do this, you're in the game to the showdown, and must place your cards face down to the left of the betting areas *after* you have made the bet. This signifies to the dealer that you are "in the game." If you do not do this, you will automatically lose your mandatory ante bet, as well as your $1 bet for the progressive and bonus-pay jackpots (provided you made that optional $1 bet).

Optional $1 Progressive Jackpot and Bonus Pay Bet

This is the $1 side bet. You do not have to make it, but it is highly advisable to do so, since you cannot win the jackpot, nor any of the bonus pays, if you do not make this side bet. You make this bet by placing your white $1 chip into the slot mounted on the playing table directly in front of the ante bet area. This slot is nearest the dealer in front of you. This mechanical device automatically drops the chip into the tray below the table once the dealer presses the requisite button to start the game (don't be concerned with these procedures for the dealer—they are automatic and the dealers will gladly explain them if you ask). Once the chip drops below, a little red light above the chip slot lights up, signifying that you are in the jackpot and bonus pay game.

Okay, now you know how to make a bet. What happens next?

How the Game Is Played

Dealers used to shuffle the cards themselves and then deal out each hand of five cards to the players in turn, left-to-right of the dealer's position. However, in almost all casinos now a shuffling machine is used. This machine shuffles each deck automatically, then deals out sets of five cards once all the players have made their required ante bets and optional jackpot bets. The dealer then simply picks up each set of five cards and spreads them face down in front of each player who has made the required bets. The dealer keeps the final set of five cards, then turns the topmost dealer's card face up, with the remaining four dealer's cards being below that card, face down. This doesn't mean much, but it does let you see one of the dealer's cards. Once this is done, the dealer resets the machine; it will proceed to shuffle the second deck to get ready for the next round. Now all the players can look at their cards.

Remember that this game plays as a five-card-draw poker game, but *without* any draw! The five cards you are dealt are *all* the cards you will get. Therefore, whatever poker hand these five cards make is the hand you're stuck with. Dealer's cards don't factor in your winning hand as they do in Double-Down Stud or Let It Ride, whereby the dealer's cards are common cards to all players. In Caribbean Stud, the five cards you hold are the *only* cards you will get for that hand. You will win or lose based entirely upon the relative strength of these cards, versus whatever cards the dealer has.

To stay in the hand thereafter, you must make a bet in the bet box below the ante box, and this bet has to be twice the ante bet amount. If you think your hand can beat the dealer, you do this, then place your five cards face down to the left of this bet and wait to see what happens. If you do not want to do this, simply throw your cards toward the dealer over and above your ante bet area. This surrenders your ante and progressive bets. The dealer will collect the ante bet (the progressive bet is already gone down the chute, providing you had made it), and moves on to other players. Once all players at the table have decided whether to bet or not, the dealer will then turn over the dealer's cards. To win your bet, two things must happen.

First, the dealer must qualify. "Qualifying" is a rule of

the game for the dealer. The dealer's cards *must* be at least ace-king—or better! If the dealer does *not* have ace-king or better, the dealer will simply pay ante bets to all players who are still in the hand at this point, and take their cards without looking at them. This is the point where your $1 progressive bet comes into play in the most important fashion. *If* your hand contains a flush or better—including the jackpot pays of straight flush and royal flush—and the dealer did *not* qualify, and you *did* make the $1 jackpot bet, you *must* tell the dealer that you have a "bonus hand." If you *do not* tell the dealer this when you have such a hand and the dealer does not qualify, the dealer will *not* look at your cards, and you will lose the winnings to which you would have been entitled. This is very important to remember.

Second, if the dealer *does* qualify with ace-king or better, the dealer will then turn over all players' cards right-to-left of the dealer's position—for those players who are still in the hand to that point. If the player's hand beats the dealer's hand, the player is paid in accordance with the pay-off hierarchy, as the following chart shows.

HAND		PAYS
One pair	=	1:1 (even money)
Two pairs	=	2:1
Three of a kind	=	3:1
Straight	=	4:1
Flush	=	5:1
Full house	=	7:1
Four of a kind	=	20:1
Straight flush	=	50:1
Royal flush	=	100:1

Remember that you get these payoffs *only* if the dealer qualifies and if your hand beats the dealer's hand. If this is so, you get paid accordingly that many times your bet, plus even money on your ante bet.

Bonus Pays

In addition to the regular pays, you can also get bonus pays. These are paid whether or not the dealer qualifies, but in order to get paid on them you must make the $1 jackpot side bet, then you must stay in the hand till showdown, and you must tell the dealer you have one of these hands if such a hand was dealt to you. These bonus pays are as follows:

Flush	$50
Full house	$75
Four of a kind	$100 (some casinos pay $500 for this, and that is best)
Straight flush	10% of the progressive jackpot, as shown on the meter.
Royal flush	100% of the progressive jackpot, as shown on the meter.

Many casinos will pay $500 for any four of a kind. These are the casinos where you should play, and you should never play in casinos that do not pay at least this much for this hand. As I have said many times, if you find a casino that slightly alters some pays among what is generally the traditionally understood pay table, this often means that there are also other alterations elsewhere in the pay scale, or other subtle alterations to the game. Casinos that do this usually also alter other pays, as well as other games. Any time you find something like this example of a reduced pay, it can be an indication that this casino also fudges with other pays as well, including those on some of their other games. This is, of course, not always so, but it is a useful guideline. It's a caution, kind of like a red flag, that you should be wary and watch out. Take a step back and look around for other subtle alterations, or changes to games and rules. It costs you nothing to do a little snooping and investigating. Ask questions.

Find out what you can. If you don't find anything else, then make your choice accordingly. Most of the time, experience will prove to you that if you find one rotten apple in a barrel, chances are the others are also infected and can be rotten to the core. I have learned to be careful. When I see one worm, I want to see if there are others around before I take a bite out of that apple. So it is with gambling games, and pays. It doesn't take much to turn a good game into a very bad one.

House Edge

Caribbean Stud Poker, and the progressive version that is the subject of this chapter, are negative expectation games. This is because the game is structured in a manner that always ensures a house advantage. On the base game, the house holds around 5.2 percent on the average. If a perfect strategy is played, this edge can be reduced to about 2.6 percent. The problem is, however, that what can be described as a "perfect" strategy is all but impossible to actually play in the real casinos and under actual conditions. It is a mathematically sound strategy, but workable only under laboratory and theoretical conditions, so it is largely useless if your purpose is to play this game for the two hours or so you wish to play in the casino today. Otherwise, playing Caribbean Stud as a means of professional play isn't viable. Therefore, anything that I will state by means of a strategy will be confined to the "workability principle," as I have outlined it in my other books.

The "progressive" feature that has made this game so popular in major casinos not only adds an element of "slots" to the game, but also increases the house edge. On the progressive side bet, the house edge is around 26.5 percent, on the average. Most casinos will hold about 18 percent to 19 percent on that feature, largely to make up for the "seed" money they put up to start the progressive feature. In most casinos, this initial seed money, as this casino investment in the game is called, starts at around $10,000 or $20,000. The casino gets paid back this money from the house edge on this bet and thereafter continues to make profits. About 71 cents out of every dollar spent on the progressive feature goes to the jackpot meter, and the rest goes to the casino. It is a very lucrative and profitable game for the casinos.

There is, however, a bigger problem when trying to calculate the various house edges for this game. Is the house edge to be calculated from merely the initial ante wager? Or is the total "element of risk" featured in this debate? What of the risk factor when the player decides to place the bet after receiving the cards, and now also adds twice the ante amount to the wager? How is that to factor in the equation? And what about that side bet, the progressive? How does that figure in the overall house edge? And what about the application of any strategy—does that affect the house edge? If so, how and by how much? This is what makes the game hard to define, and also volatile. Different versions of this game are played in various casinos, with different rules. Some don't play the progressive, while others do and pay more, or pay less. Various online versions also make the game slightly different.

Basically, the best way to look at it is purely from the "single-wager" perspective. If you are playing at a $5 table, this means that your ante bet will be $5 minimum. This also means that you will be wagering $10 in the bet box, if you choose to continue with the hand. Assuming also that you are playing the progressive feature, you also add the cost of that $1 for the progressive into the bet. Thus, your single-wager concept is $16 per hand (let us not get confused here by applications of any strategy that would make us fold and forfeit the ante and progressive bet, for this example). Your risk factor is $16 per hand. Of that, the $15 faces a house edge of around 5.2 percent (having grouped the bets, as I've said, for the sake of this example). The $1 bet faces a house edge of about 26.5 percent. Put this all together as a single-wager group, and you are facing the house edge of (5.2) + (26.5) ÷ (3) = 10.57. I used the division factor of 3, because we have three bets—the ante, the bet, and the progressive—each with an added risk exposure. This isn't meant to be scientific, but merely instructional to try to gauge just exactly how badly we can be exposed to financial risk. By using this formula to clarify the *totality of the group bet* and its resultant risk exposure, we can say with a fair degree of educated assumption that the overall house advantage in this kind of a game will be around 10.57 percent over all events and wagers combined as one group, allowing for the inclusion of the risk exposure.

Don't try to analyze this mathematically, because this is only an example to allow us to better understand the totality of the financial risk in the game. What I have done here should show that Progressive Caribbean Stud is not a game that can successfully be classified among the better casino games, and that all the bets in this game combined will generally yield a high house edge. That is all I have tried to show here by means of these examples.

Where to Play

Many casinos in the United States, and elsewhere, play various versions of this game. Without trying to classify them all, and since I live in Las Vegas, the following chart shows those casinos in Las Vegas that have this game, and what the average per-wager house edge is generally to be found on this game in those casinos, as calculated by the *traditional* method of basing the game's house edge on the initial bet.

CASINO	HOUSE EDGE (%)
Bally's, Paris, California, Las Vegas Club, Hilton	5.8
Luxor, Excalibur, Mandalay Bay, Monte Carlo	5.8
Bellagio, Venetian, Rio, Harrah's, Circus Circus	5.2
Flamingo Hilton, Imperial Palace	5.2

These are only rounded figures, and based only on the ante bets, and affected only by the reduced pays in some situations. The house edge on the progressive feature is in the range of 18 percent to 29 percent and depends on the jackpot structure and pays. Casinos listed in the last two lines of the chart above pay $500 for the four of a kind, while the casinos in the first two lines only pay $100 for that same pay. Although this doesn't factor into the overall house edge—because these bets are paid from the progressive meter and not from the house edge on the base game—you can clearly see this one key item tends to show that something else has been tweaked, as I've suggested earlier. It's simply a good rule of thumb to look first at the bonus jackpot pays of the four of a kind, and then see if the rest of the pay table has been changed as well, especially if some of the standard pays on the base game have also been altered. All of it will mean less money for you, and more for the casino, if these pays are less than they should be.

Simple Strategy

Progressive Caribbean Stud is a difficult game to quantify and to play with any kind of a workable strategy, but the suggestions I have compiled here will make it easier for you to book some good wins, and lose less, during your short-term exposure to this game. I will, however, caution you against choosing this as one of your main games to play. Although the wins can be big if you are lucky to overcome that huge house edge and hit the jackpot, the game is too volatile to play often and regularly. By all means, try it, and have fun with it, but save the majority of your gaming investment for better and more lucrative games, such as blackjack, Craps, live poker, and, yes, roulette. Even roulette is better than Caribbean Stud, and certainly no worse (roulette holds an average 5.26 percent for the house, while most Caribbean Stud games hold an average 5.2 percent. That is quite close, but roulette can be a faster game and a lot more fun). Therefore, here are my recommendations for a basic strategy for Progressive Caribbean Stud, as played in major U.S. casinos.

- Don't expect to win big at this game *without* playing the $1 side bet! To play Caribbean Stud without the $1 side bet is financial suicide. *Always* make your $1 side bet. While this side bet—considered alone—contains the greatest portion of the house edge in this game, remember my combined-wager principle. Bucking this high house edge on this bet may look like a bad idea when considered singly, but when you combine all the factors of the game, along with your objective to win big money fast, playing this game without this side bet option—regardless of its high house edge— doesn't make sense. What would you do if you didn't play that $1 and hit a hand that would have paid you $200,000, and instead paid you only $5 for the ante? This is the point that is often lost in strategy advice that is given by mathematicians, or by those who analyze games purely from the mathematical perspective. Yes, mathematically speaking the $1 side bet is a horrendous bet, and one that should be avoided—but that is entirely wrong in the real world. Although the theory clearly shows that this is a statistically bad bet, how good is that advice if it costs you the jackpot?

- Don't bluff. If your hand isn't at least a pair of something, don't even think about staying in the hand. Many players will habitually stay in every hand, or try to play marginal hands such as ace-king-queen, or even pair-twos, in order to win their ante bet. This is a borderline bluff and means (on a $5 minimum table) you are risking $16 to win $5! A lousy bet indeed. Don't do this. If your hand is at least a pair of threes, or better, stay in the hand. Otherwise throw in, take your loss, and play the next hand.
- If you are dealt a bonus pay hand, *always* tell the dealer immediately. Say something like, "I have a bonus hand." Don't be intimidated by other players who may smirk at you, or even dealers who look bored or give you funny looks. You're not there to entertain them—you are there to *win money*! It's the rule, so say it!
- Never, ever—I mean *never*—play this game *without* the $1 jackpot bet. I know I've already said this above, but it bears repeating. Horror stories about people who did *not* do this abound. Here's one of them:

A while back in Las Vegas one of the casinos had a jackpot on Caribbean Stud of more than $200,000. That's a lot of money in anyone's language. A woman in her mid-fifties sat down at the game and refused to put in the extra $1, even though she had plenty of money and was betting well over the table minimum bet requirement. All players at the table, myself included, as well as the dealers and the pit staff, tried to explain to her the advantages of the side bet. She refused. Four hands later she was dealt a natural royal flush. The dealer did *not* qualify, and she did *not* have the $1 jackpot bet. So, instead of receiving over $200,000, all she won was $25 for her ante bet (she was betting $25 ante with a $50 bet behind). Let this be a lesson to you if you ever plan on playing this game. It's fun to play, but if you play it, play it to win and not to lose, as this woman did.

• Find a casino where the jackpot has grown at least to over $80,000. Playing this game where the jackpot is not this high simply means that the jackpot was hit recently and that all players will be feeding the meter for a long time. Don't waste your money. Go to another casino. Casinos usually seed the game with either $10,000 or $20,000, to start it off. Give yourself an advantage and ask the pit boss what the seed amount of the jackpot is. He will tell you, and if he doesn't, go over his head. By law they have to give you this information, so don't be shy about asking. By knowing the amount of the house seed money for the jackpot in that casino, you will be better able to make a judgment about the jackpot's odds. For example, if the jackpot meter is at $80,000, and the seed money the casino provides is $10,000, then you know this jackpot is laying you 8:1 odds for your money. It's kind of like pot odds in live poker—the better the pot odds, the more likely a call should be made in marginal situations. Similarly, the better the jackpot odds are in this game, relative to the seed money, the more viable the game is for your investment, even if such an investment is only a few dollars for a short while at the game. To understand this even better, what if you asked the pit boss in this casino what the seed money was, and he said $20,000? In this case the $80,000 jackpot would be laying you 4:1 on your money. Yes, I understand that this is not the way to break down the odds relative to your investment as far as a mathematical analysis is concerned, but it is a very useful way to judge whether or not you should play this game in this casino, as opposed to another. That is all I am trying to achieve with this example—a simple means to help you calculate where to invest your gaming dollars. Just as looking for the $500 payoff on the four of a kind is a good rule of thumb to see if this is a good game for you, similarly this method of calculating what the jackpot is laying you is another means by which you can make such a quick determination. Put all of this together, and you will be better off and make more informed and more intelligent choices. In the long run, as well as short term, these simple considerations will save you money. This is not a "cheap" game—this game is very expensive, because of the high house edge over all events, as well as the combined events. Using these simple principles will help you avoid spending more than you would have otherwise and give you a better chance at more "value" pays.

• Play in a casino that offers a $500 bonus pay for any four of a kind, instead of $100. Many casinos will do this, so search them out. A few phone calls will do the trick. Also ask them at what level the jackpot is. If the casino pays $500 for any four of a kind *and* its jackpot is more than $80,000, that's the place you ought to be.

• Don't be disappointed when you receive great hands, but the dealer does not qualify. This happens often, and that's why this game is so good for the house. But it can be good for you, too. Eventually, you will get good hands, and when you do they'll often come in bunches. You're at this game to win, so stick to it.

• Which brings us to the size of your bankroll. For a $3 minimum game (which I will *not* advise you to play), a good bankroll is $150. For a $5 minimum game (the best for the game), a good bankroll is $300. For games with ante bets of $10 or more, a bankroll of $500 to $1,000 is a good stake. Sounds like a lot of money? Not really—you must invest some to win some. If you can't afford this stake, play another game until you win, or save up before you sit down. Don't play under-capitalized. If you do, you'll lose. I can tell you from direct experience that Caribbean Stud can separate you from your money very quickly, and unless you have the required bankroll, you will not win. However, you can, and *will,* win a sizable amount of money if you have the necessary bankroll with you, and the patience to stick it out until you get the hands you need. I have invested $600 on many occasions, and after several hours came away from the game with a $1,600 *profit!* But it takes time, money, and patience.

• Position at the table. If you can, sit at the dealer's far left (to the far right as you face the table). This position will *always* get the first hand out. In this seat, the order of cards dealt to you will *never* alter. In every other seat this is not so, since as players come and go your cards will change in the order received. So, if you were getting very good hands, but the player in front of you in the order of dealing was getting lousy hands, and that player leaves, *you* will now be getting that player's lousy cards, and the player behind you in order of dealing will now be getting your good cards. This is not so in the number one seat, where no matter how many other players sit down or leave at that table, your cards will never be changed because of changes in position dealing.

Crunching Numbers for Caribbean Stud

I understand that many players would rather dive right into the game and play; however, I think that a little more detail may provide an added edge in making more subtly meaningful decisions. The above strategy for Caribbean Stud is probably all you will need in order to gain the maximum enjoyment of the game; there is more to this game than meets the eye, or that would be discussed when trying to explain the game simply. For that reason, I also wish to provide you with a few additional charts. Figure 9 shows the *net* pays for Caribbean Stud, and the various combinations and probability that these entail.

Figure 9

A chart demonstrating the possible outcomes for Caribbean Stud, the *net* return per initial bet, the probability, and the total return.

Numbers for Caribbean Stud

HAND	NET PAYS	COMBINATIONS	TOTAL RETURN	PROBABILITY	AVERAGE RETURN
Ace/king	3	18,505,682,208	55,517,046,624	0.00092838	0.00278515
Pair	3	2,324,742,321,600	6,974,226,964,800	0.11662647	0.34987941
Two pairs	5	488,012,139,360	2,440,060,696,800	0.02448234	0.12241170
Three of a kind	7	234,242,908,320	1,639,700,358,240	0.01175138	0.08225964
Straight	9	43,805,516,100	394,249,644,900	0.00219761	0.01977851
Flush	11	21,856,990,280	240,426,893,080	0.00109651	0.01206161
Full house	15	16,624,475,280	249,367,129,200	0.00083401	0.01251012
Four of a kind	41	2,832,435,800	116,129,867,800	0.0001421	0.00582594
Straight flush	101	156,929,720	15,849,901,720	0.00000787	0.00079515
Royal flush	201	16,759,740	3,368,707,740	0.00000084	0.00016900
Ante only	1	4,532,514,033,720	4,532,514,033,720	0.22738482	0.22738482
Push	0	321,623,100	0	0.00001614	0
Fold	-1	9,523,005,974,460	-9,523,005,974,460	-0.47774524	-0.47774524
Dealer wins	-3	2,726,592,727,512	-8,179,778,182,536	0.13678629	-0.41035888
Total		19,933,230,517,200	-1,041,372,912,372	1	-0.05224306

You will now be able to learn not only what the game's payoff chart is, or the game's payback percentage, but what the game's actual hand-by-hand *net* result is. This "net" is the true amount of money you will get on those hands—or won't get on the events shown in "negative" minus indicators. Use this chart to help you make your own determinations as to how you play the game, and each hand in the game, relative to the rules of the game as they may be posted in the casino where you are playing. For example, you may see that the four of a kind is listed as a 20:1 payoff, but from this chart you can easily see that your average net pay on this event is actually only an average of forty-one units. This is only a tad higher than 2:1. It all depends on the payoff, and please note that this does not include the progressive amount. For casinos that pay $500 for a four of a kind, this will alter the numbers with a greater net gain. However, since most casinos will pay this only from the progressive meter, with the base pay being only $100 for the four of a kind (or the stated amount as the case may be in the casino where you are playing), Figure 10 (page 132) shows what the numbers are for the progressive bet.

Okay, now that you can see what the net gain (or loss) may be on those hands, what about your expectation? What can you possibly hope to get from these hands? Remember that we are here concentrating on the net gain and expected return as based on the progressive side bet in the game. As I've mentioned earlier, the casinos will traditionally keep about 25 percent to 30 percent of all the drop money that results from players making that extra $1 side wager to qualify for the progressive. Although this means that the average house edge on this bet is usually around 26.5 percent, the question you should ask is: At what point can the players expect an even proposition? Basically, at what point in the growth of the jackpot will the players gain an equal bet? Additionally, at what point can the players expect a positive payback situation? Well, these questions are answered in Figure 11 (pages 132–33).

Using the same charts for the casinos as that used in Figure 10, here we see that for casinos that use the payback hierarchy of these varying tables, the break-even point is different, as is the progression toward a player-positive expectation from the game. For example, in Casino 1 the break-even point for the players is when the jackpot grows to $263,205, while in Casino 4 the same point is reached at only $176,613. This again serves to show the vast differences in player payback expectation among the various casino payoffs. The same applies to the other items in this chart, and to the overall approach to the game. As we have seen for other games throughout this book, there is a lot more to all casino gambling games than just the simple act of placing a wager and hoping to win something. Hoping to win what? How much? What will it cost? What's the payback? How much will I have to wager before I can hope to gain an advantage? Can I get an advantage? How high does the jackpot have to grow before it overcomes the casino's edge on the bet? And so on for this game, as well as all the others. Viewed from within the mathematical model, it is even more important to recognize the value of the math in pointing the way toward understanding the casino games and the strategy you wish to apply. Though I maintain that mathematics alone isn't the total answer, nor the only one, I have also said that it is an extremely useful guideline in all matters of gambling. This is demonstrated in these figures for Progressive Caribbean Stud, and particularly so for the extra side bet feature.

There is, however, a vast difference between what is the mathematically correct decision and what is personally and profitably the correct decision. Mathematically, the side bet in Progressive Caribbean Stud is a deadly bad bet. If you have ever played this game you know how rare it is that any

132

Figure 10

The varying payoffs that are available in different casinos for the same hands.

Payoff Schedules for Progressive Caribbean Stud Side Bets Among Various Casinos

HAND	CASINO 1	CASINO 2	CASINO 3	CASINO 4	CASINO 5	CASINO 6	CASINO 7
Royal flush	100%	100%	100%	100%	100%	100%	100%
Straight flush	10%	10%	10%	10%	10%	10%	10%
Four of a kind	$100	$150	$500	$500	$500	$500	$500
Full house	$75	$100	$100	$150	$75	$100	$150
Flush	$50	$50	$50	$75	$50	$75	$100

Figure 11

The jackpot level for the paybacks to reach
a break-even point, or become a player-positive exectation.

Expected Payback for Progressive Caribbean Stud Side Bets Among Various Casinos

AVERAGE (%)	CASINO 1	CASINO 2	CASINO 3	CASINO 4	CASINO 5	CASINO 6	CASINO 7
5	-61,665	-78,086	-106,823	-148,257	-94,507	-123,625	-165,059
10	-44,566	-60,987	-89,724	-131,158	-77,408	-106,527	-147,961
15	-27,468	-43,889	-72,626	-114,060	-60,310	-89,428	-130,863
20	-10,369	-26,791	-55,527	-96,962	-43,212	-72,330	-113,764
25	6,729	-9,692	-38,429	-79,863	-26,113	-55,232	-96,666

Figure 11 (cont.)

The jackpot level for the paybacks to reach
a break-even point, or become a player-positive exectation.

Expected Payback for Progressive Caribbean Stud Side Bets Among Various Casinos

AVERAGE (%)	CASINO 1	CASINO 2	CASINO 3	CASINO 4	CASINO 5	CASINO 6	CASINO 7
30	23,827	7,406	-21,331	-62,765	-9,015	-38,133	-79,567
35	40,926	24,505	-4,232	-45,666	8,084	-21,035	-62,469
40	58,024	41,603	12,866	-28,568	25,182	-3,936	-45,371
45	75,123	58,702	29,965	-11,469	42,281	13,162	-28,272
50	92,221	75,800	47,063	5,629	59,379	30,261	-11,174
55	109,319	92,898	64,162	22,727	76,477	47,359	5,925
60	126,418	109,997	81,260	39,826	93,576	64,457	23,023
65	143,516	127,095	98,358	56,924	110,674	81,556	40,122
70	160,615	144,194	115,457	74,023	127,773	98,654	57,220
75	177,713	161,292	132,555	91,121	144,871	115,753	74,318
80	194,812	178,391	149,654	108,219	161,969	132,851	91,417
85	211,910	195,489	166,752	125,318	179,068	149,949	108,515
90	229,008	212,587	183,851	142,416	196,166	167,048	125,614
95	246,107	229,686	200,949	159,515	213,265	184,146	142,712
100	263,205	246,784	218,047	176,613	230,363	201,245	159,811
105	280,304	263,883	235,146	193,712	247,462	218,343	176,909
110	297,402	280,981	252,244	210,810	264,560	235,442	194,007
115	314,501	298,079	269,343	227,908	281,658	252,540	211,106
120	331,599	315,178	286,441	245,007	298,757	269,638	228,20
125	348,697	332,276	303,539	262,105	315,855	286,737	245,303

of the jackpots grow to over $195,000, which would be just about the break-even point for this side bet in the average casino. This means that for the majority of players, and the possible majority of instances that you will play this game, you and these players will most likely be playing the game in a situation that is a decidedly negative expectation. This adds to your overall costs of the game, and it is for this reason that Caribbean Stud is among those games that are rarely selected as part of any professional, or semiprofessional, approach to gambling. Nevertheless, for the traditionally average player, who is exposed to the game once or twice a year, the point of personal profitability remains— don't play the game without the side bet, regardless of what the mathematics may say. As long as you can find a Caribbean Stud table where the progressive is at least $80,000 you can get at least a marginally decent game. Even though at that level the game's side bet is far from being a mathematically viable option, that doesn't belie the question of "what if?" Statistics are only useful when "all things are equal." Well, all things *aren't* always equal, not in the real world and not in statistical models. Anomalies abound everywhere. What if one of those anomalies hits you while you sit at the Progressive Caribbean Stud table. Remember the example of the $200,000 jackpot in Las Vegas that I mentioned earlier? Therein lies the point of the simple strategy: Know the mathematics, know the odds and percentages, use them as your guidelines to profitable gambling, but also learn to know when to deviate from them, and why. And that, dear friends, is the story of Progressive Caribbean Stud poker in a nutshell.

6

Double Down Stud

Double Down Stud is a relatively new game, approved by the Gaming Control Board a few years ago as a table game and also as a video game. It is played in only a few casinos, but is becoming more popular. Casinos in Reno have this game, but it is still rare in Las Vegas. This game reflects Texas Hold'Em more than Five-Card Stud, and differs from Caribbean Stud because of its structure, increased simplicity, high payoffs for the player, and also because it has no progressive. The game is played on a blackjack-style table and begins with the player making a bet in the bet box directly in front of her. The cards are shuffled by machine, single deck, and the players receive one card each, face up. The dealer then deals himself four cards, three face up and one face down. The players have the option of doubling their bets by placing another bet in the double down box directly behind their bet box. The double down amount has to equal the bet. After all bets are made, the dealer turns up the last card and winners are paid and losers taken.

INTRODUCTION TO DOUBLE DOWN STUD

Similar to Hold'Em poker, in this game the players use their one card to make winning combinations first out of the three dealer's cards they see plus the one card dealt to them, and, in the end, out of all the five cards viewed. The dealer's four cards are common cards to all players, and the dealer does not play. All wins and losses are determined by the pay-off schedule shown in the following chart.

Pay Table for Double Down Stud

HAND	PAYS
Royal flush	2,000 to 1
Straight flush	200 to 1
Four of a kind	50 to 1
Full house	11 to 1
Flush	8 to 1
Straight	5 to 1
Three of a kind	3 to 1
Two pairs	2 to 1
Pair of jacks or better	1 to 1
Pair of 6s or better	Push

Basically, this is a video poker game played on a table, much like Caribbean Stud. The disadvantage for the player is that it offers *no draw*. The big *advantage* to the player is the ability to double the bet when the player can see, first hand, that he already has a winner. The player has this considerable advantage in that he can immediately see whether he has a winner or not, and if so, to double the bet with no risk of losing. And the house can expect a steady 2.67 percent profit potential, so it's a good game all around.

Game Rules

- Each hand is dealt from a freshly shuffled single deck.
- Players make the initial bet.
- The dealer then gives each player one card face up, and deals four community cards—three up and one down.
- Each player has the option to double his bet or not.
- The dealer turns over the down card.

Simple Strategy

These are the simplest and most profitable hands on which you should double your bet:

- Any pat hand of a pair of 6s or greater
- Four to a flush, straight flush, or royal flush
- Four to any outside straight
- Unsuited J-Q-K-A

This is a very simple game. If, after you see the first four cards you have a pair of 6s or better, you know that you can't lose, and therefore the additional bet is not at risk. You have much to gain and little to lose. The game becomes more volatile when you have a draw to a straight, or a flush, or the straight flush and royal flush. Then you have to decide whether or not you want to risk the extra bet. My advice is, always do so for any flush, straight flush or royal flush draw, but *not* for a straight—with the exception of the unsuited J-Q-K-A, because that hand contains no house edge at all. Any other combination means that you already have a winner, so go and double down. If played properly the risk factor is only between 2 percent and 3 percent.

House Edge

The house edge on the table version of Double Down Stud is 2.67 percent. That's all there is to this game, and it can be quite fun and profitable.

Video Double Down Stud

The video version, now available in several casinos, is a little different. Video Double Down Stud poker is a regular video poker machine, but instead of dealing five cards after the player deposits his coins, Double Down Stud machines deal four cards face up, for the player to see, and the fifth card face down. The player then has the choice of doubling his bet, or not. As in the table game, the advantage to the player is that if he sees an automatic winner on the first four cards dealt by the machine, he risks nothing by doubling his bet. On the video version this is accomplished by pressing the "double" button. If the player has credits on the machine's meter, the machine will automatically deduct the same number of credits equal to the player's original bet. The final card is then turned over. If it improves the hand, the player is paid accordingly. If not, the player is paid according to the value of the wining hand made on the first four cards dealt.

The benefits of video Double Down Stud are the larger payoffs. For example: On a regular video poker machine, a four of a kind will pay 125 coins for a five-coin bet. On the Double Down Stud version, if the player doubles his bet, a four of a kind will pay 500 coins, for a five-coin initial bet, with a five-coin double down. This is quite good, more so because the advantage is with the player in this event. If you are dealt three of a kind on the first four cards drawn by the machine, you already know you have a winner, so the player risks nothing by doubling the bet. If the last card makes your hand into a four of a kind, you're in the money big time! The same applies to all the other payoffs on the video Double Down Stud. And if you are dealt a four of a kind immediately on the first four cards, you're in the money big time because you know you can't lose, and doubling this bet then makes you a really big winner.

The bad news is that paying hands do not occur with the same frequency as, say, on a regular 9-6 Jacks or Better video poker machine. Players do not get as many paying hands. But the upside is that when you *do* get a paying hand, even a pair of jacks-or-better will pay twenty coins, as opposed to only five coins on the regular video poker machines. Double Down Stud machines pay even money for a pair of 6s through 10s. For these reasons, both the video version and the table version of Double Down Stud are among the better games for your gaming investment. They can get a trifle boring at times, so I'd advise you to give them a try for a short slice of your gaming time, say an hour or less, and then move on, unless you are winning, in which case you should stay and maximize that winning cycle. Also, some of the newest video versions of this game are now progressives, and this means that if you hit the royal flush, you will be paid the top progressive jackpot, with the doubled bet. This also contributes to making this game one of the better casino games, overall.

There is virtually no strategy for this game, simple or otherwise. If you are playing the table game version, you only need to remember that if you already have 6s or better, you should double your bet because you can't lose. Otherwise, don't, unless you have a draw to a big hand, such as a flush or a straight, or a straight flush or a royal flush. Any other combination, including draws to four of a kind and full house hands, means that you already have a pair or trips. If this is the case you either already have a winning hand, or a very good draw to one, so the double down option becomes viable. In the video game version, the same applies. If among the first four cards you see you already have a pair of 6s or better, you can't lose, so double down. The same strategy applies to the draws.

And that's about as simple as it gets. I describe the video version of this game in more detail in my book *Powerful Profits from Video Poker.*

Pai Gow Poker

Pai Gow Poker is one casino game that doesn't get the popularity and appreciation it deserves. Many die-hard poker players dismiss this game as "poker by name only." To some extent this is true. Pai Gow Poker isn't *really* a game of poker at all—it merely uses the rules of poker, in its own particular version, to determine the value of hands. Other than that, the game possesses few of the "real poker" characteristics. Little of the traditional poker skill is involved in playing Pai Gow Poker. For instance, bluffing hasn't nearly as much value to the player as the same skillfully applied practice would have in a traditional poker game. This is so because there are no betting rounds to go by, nor are there any rules of play that would allow one player to exploit a "tell" from another. Winning and losing hands are determined solely on the no-draw value of cards initially dealt, as positioned by the player in the "high hand" and "low hand" categories, versus the same arrangement as performed by the "banker." Nevertheless, Pai Gow Poker is a very interesting game from several perspectives. It's almost like a combination of craps, baccarat, blackjack, and poker.

INTRODUCTION TO PAI GOW POKER

The game is played with a single deck of cards that includes a joker. The joker is used either as an ace, or to make a straight or a flush. Seven hands are dealt, each containing seven cards, as in Seven-Card Stud. A cup containing three dice is then shaken, and the resulting roll of the dice determines the position of the hands, starting from the banker's hand. (In some casinos, an automatic shuffling machine has replaced the dealer in the dealing of the hands, and an automated position selection device is used to replace the dice shaker to determine position of hands to be dealt.) Each player on the table then receives a hand. In front of each player are two boxes, one marked high hand, and the other second highest. The object is to take the seven cards and divide them into a high hand of five cards and a low hand of two cards. Stud poker rules are used, the only variation being that in Pai Gow Poker you need to beat the dealer with *both* hands, high and low, in order to win. For instance: your hand has A-joker-10-10-7-8-6 (forget the suits for the sake of this example). If this was stud poker this hand could be played as a 10-high straight (allowing the wild joker as the missing 9). In Pai Gow Poker this is a strong hand allowing several variations (see the following chart)—remember that the joker can be used as an ace, or to make a straight.

HIGH HAND—FIVE CARDS	LOW HAND—TWO CARDS
A-Joker-7-8-6	10-10
or	
6-7-8-Joker-10	A-10

Any two pairs in Pai Gow Poker, particularly with aces, is a strong hand. However, as most house rules testify, the idea is to make two strong hands. Caesars Palace in Las Vegas uses the ace-up rule variation. This means that whenever the house has an ace option with a strong high hand, they will use the ace for the low hand and take the stronger high hand. In the above example the 10-10 low hand and the ace-ace high hand are two strong hands, but by applying the ace-up rule, it is better to take the straight with the ace-10 as the low hand.

With an ace up, the only way the dealer can beat your hand is if he has an ace-10 or better, including a pair as low hand—rare in Pai Gow Poker. But your straight as the high hand is even stronger, and as play will testify, at most times any hand with two pairs or better as the high hand is a winner most of the time. Playing ace up and taking the straight, as in this example, is playing it safe. That's why the house rules use it. In Pai Gow Poker you push, or "tie," a lot of hands. If you beat the dealer with one hand, either high or low, but he beats you with the other, it's a push—a stand-off—a tie. You don't lose and you don't win. The house rules employ the ace-up rule in order to minimize house losses, since this way they will push the table more often than lose. As a player, however, the above example offers you the choice of the two ways of playing the hand. In this case the 10-10 low hand with the ace-joker high hand is the better way to play. The ace-up low hand and the straight high hand are safer, but then you aren't playing for a tie, you are playing to win.

Pai Gow Poker is similar to Seven-Card Stud in that it uses standard poker rules to determine value of hands, but that's where the similarity ends. As we saw with the above example, standards of play to Seven-Card Stud rules do not apply. Merely the method for selecting values of hands is used (i.e., straight, flush, pair, two pairs). How you *play* the hands is determined by Pai Gow Poker rules, and these are many with many more variances. Basically, though, the idea is simple: take the highest hand possible out of seven cards and place it as the high hand. Then take the next highest hand and place it as the low hand. If you beat both the dealer's hands, you win. Pai Gow Poker is similar to blackjack in respect to "pushes" or "ties." In blackjack when you have, say, 18, and the dealer has 18, it's a standoff. Neither wins. Same in Pai Gow Poker: if you beat the dealer with one hand, and he beats you with the other, it's a tie.

Baccarat also makes a presence in that the bank is offered to each player in turn, the wins are all even money, and the house takes a 5 percent commission. But in Pai Gow Poker when you bank, you bank not only against the house, but also against all the players at the table. So, if you are going to bank, make sure you can carry the bankroll necessary to pay off all the bets should you lose. If you bank, you become the casino. In some card rooms—not traditional casinos—the bank is offered to players, or bought by players, in much the same way as European baccarat games are often played where the banker is any player who has won the bank, or bought it from another player. That player will hold the bank and bank the game for as long as she is winning, or until she decides to sell the bank to another player. These situations, however, can vary from card club to card club. For the simplicity of this introductory chapter, we will use the Las Vegas Rules as the basis for explaining the game.

Craps also makes an appearance in Pai Gow Poker, but only marginally. The use of the dice often seems puzzling to people not familiar with the game, but it's not difficult to understand. The three dice in the cup are "tossed" simply to determine positions of the hands being dealt to the players and the dealer. Banker is always 8 or 15, and the cards are therefore distributed to players right-to-left of dealer's position—taking into account what the cumulative number of the three-dice roll was.

Pai Gow Poker can be a slow game. It is not unusual to push several hands in a row. Because the variations of hands are so many, the selections often make for a one-hand winner and a one-hand loser, in which case it becomes a tie—push. But it's a very interesting and stimulating game, and one you can play for a long time without losing your whole bankroll in a few minutes, as you can in Craps or blackjack if you have a bad run—or even in traditional poker if you catch that streak in which the player at the end of the table always fishes out a better hand on the last turn. As with all other casino games, selection of hands and opportunities to maximize your bets and bank when opportune are important if you're a serious player out to win.

House Way Set

Casinos set their two hands so as to play it safe. The house wants to avoid, as often as possible, situations wherein they have to pay off a bet. Since Pai Gow Poker can also be banked by the players, not all action is always against the house as represented by the dealer. In most Las Vegas casinos, the dealer (we will now use the word "dealer" to represent the "house" in this short section) will play one hand against the players, then offer the bank to the players in turn, from dealer's left-to-right, player's right-to-left. In other casinos, any player can ask to bank at any time. Still others will allow any player to ask for the bank, but the dealer must be "bank" for at least one hand between each hand banked by a player. Some casinos won't care; as long as the player has enough chips (or money) available to bank all the bets, he can continue to be the bank for as long as he wishes.

Whenever any player is the bank, the dealer's hand represents the house, and therefore the banker's hand action is against the casino, while all other players' action is against the player acting as bank. For these reasons, it is always to the house advantage to set the house hand as safely as possible, to assure as many "pushes" as it can. That way, the house minimizes its risk of having to pay off on losing hands, and still assures itself of collecting the 5 percent vig (commission) from those hands that so qualify.

To show you how Las Vegas casinos would play, here is an example of a generic House Set of hands in Pai Gow Poker. I have "generalized" these house rules to reflect the majority of house rules in Las Vegas casinos. The "front" refers to the two-card hand I previously identified as the low hand, and the "back" refers to the five-card hand I have called the high hand. Remember that these are examples of how the casino dealers set these hands to benefit the house! You don't have to play the same way. You can set your hands more aggressively, as I have shown in my earlier example. To understand how to do this, simply follow these hands and analyze them for yourself as we analyzed my earlier example. It will quickly become clear to you how you can modify some of these hands to reflect aggressiveness for financial profits, while also using the same methods when you choose to be Banker.

For pairs and no pairs, the house set is as follows:
- *No pair:* Place the second and third highest cards in the front.
- *One pair:* Place the pair in back and the next two highest cards in the front.
- *Two pairs:* Split the two pairs except for the following three situations
  - Both pairs are 7s or less.
  - Both pairs are 10s or less plus ace.

- One pair of face cards, one pair of 6s or less, and an ace.
- *Three pairs:* Play highest pair in front.
- *Three of a kind:* Play three of a kind in back except when there are three aces, in which case keep the pair of aces and use the third ace with the ace-up rule.
- *Two three of a kinds:* Split the highest and play bigger pair up front.

For straights and flushes, the house set is as follows:
- Always play straight or flush in the high hand except when
  - There are any aces along with any other pair.
  - There are two pairs 10s or over.
  - There are two pairs 10s or under with any ace.
- With a six or seven card straight or flush, play the highest hand possible in the front while maintaining the straight or flush in the back.
- If the hand contains both a straight and a flush, play the hand in the back and put the highest hand up front, as long as the front hand is a king or better. Otherwise play the flush in the back.

For full house and four of a kind, the house set is as follows:
- *Full house:* Split, except with pair of 2s and an ace/king to be played up front.
- *Full house with three of a kind and two pairs:* Play the highest pair up front.
- *Four of a kind:* Play according to the rank of the four of a kind:
  - 2 through 6: Always keep together.
  - 7 through 10: Split unless an ace and a face card or better can be played up front.

- *Jack through king:* Split unless hand also contains a pair of 10s or higher.
- *Aces:* Split unless a pair of 7s or higher can be played up front.

For any straight flush, the house set is as follows:
- Play the straight flush in back, but play as a two pair with:
  - Aces and any other pair.
  - Both pairs 10s or higher.
  - Both pairs 10s or less and a single ace.
- Play a straight or flush instead if an ace and a face card or a pair can be played in front.

For the royal flush and five aces, the house set is as follows:
- Play the royal flush in the back, but play as a two pair with:
  - Aces and any other pair.
  - Both pairs 10s or higher.
- Break up royal flush if a straight or flush can be played in back and a king or better up front.
- *Five aces:* Split unless pair of kings can be played in front.

House Edge

The actual house edge in Pai Gow Poker depends not only on the game and where it is being played (in which region of the USA, or elsewhere in the world) but also on the casino itself and that particular casino's house rules. Such a calculation is also skill based, inasmuch as it depends on how well you set your hands. If you are a very aggressive player, and always take the win-win attitude and set your hand accordingly, then you take a greater risk. Your risk factor therefore affects the house edge on the game. Overall, if you are such a player, you could be facing a house edge greater than the average by several percentage points, or at the very least a significant fraction of a percent. On the other hand, if you are a highly conservative player, and always play the house way, exactly that same way against that house, you can actually reduce the house average edge by about 0.20 percent, or even more in some cases. There are other possibilities as well.

What if you are a great strategy player, and also know the many various ways in which the house sets its hands? Now you discover that this particular casino sets its hands in a manner with no casino advantage. You can exploit this as a house-versus-house set strategy, and actually affect the house edge on those bets to a player-positive fraction. It is a very complex situation, and the complete analysis would fill up a whole book. Therefore, to keep this as simple as possible, the following charts show the probabilities of the hand outcomes in Pai Gow Poker, and the *average* house edge percentages as they apply (using Las Vegas as an average factor, based on a game between one banker and one player).

HANDS	PROBABILITY (%)
Player wins both high and low	28.57
Push (Tie)	41.46
Banker wins both high and low	29.97

AVERAGE HOUSE EDGE	(%)
Player	2.84
Banker	0.09
Combined	1.45

The average house edge in most of these Pai Gow Poker games is about 1.45 percent, with the best of the averages being about 1.19 percent, and the worst about 1.76 percent. Aggressive players with risky hand sets can expect a higher average, while acutely conservative players can allow for a slightly lower average house edge. For all players, the probability that the low hands will tie is 2.55 percent, and the probability that the high hands will tie is 0.32 percent. You will also notice that the house edge on the player hands is highest, and that it is lowest on the banker. That is why the casinos charge a 5 percent vig on banker hands, and on winning hands against the house when the player is acting as banker. All things combined, Pai Gow Poker actually offers a very good gamble for your dollar, and at a fairly good value—especially if you have enough money to be the banker and are able to play in a casino that will allow you to bank for as long as you want.

Simple Strategy

I have already outlined some of the nuances of simple strategy and how house rules apply and affect a player's choices. Here are a few more suggestions:

• Play to win. If you have two pairs, split them, with the lower pair of the two going to the low hand and the second to the high hand. If no other combination is possible from all your cards, this is still a better way to win, rather than playing the safe way for a push, as the house plays.

• If you have two pairs of 6s and lower, but you have an ace, or a joker you are using as an ace, keep the low two pairs as the high hand and play the ace up as the low hand. Place the next highest card with the ace to make the two-card low hand.

• Never break a flush or a straight, *unless* you have at least two pairs, one of which is jacks or higher.

• If you have two pairs and are splitting them between the high and low hands, *always* place the *lower* pair as the low hand. Many players make the mistake of flip-flopping pairs, and this results in forfeiture of your bet. *Any* such mistake will forfeit your hand.

• If you have a full house in the seven cards, but no other pair, and no possibility to make a pair low hand with a flush or a straight as the high hand, *always* keep the three of a kind as the high hand and use the remaining pair as the low hand. Remember that Pai Gow Poker is *not* like regular poker. In this game a full house will do you no good if you don't have a strong enough hand as the low hand. If you had a full house of A-A-A-6-6, and the other two cards were 2-3, putting the 2-3 as your low hand will surely result in a push. A banker's 4-3 low hand will beat you, and although the full house high hand is great, what good is it if you don't win? A push is good only if you have junk, and are lucky not to lose with it. But if you split the full house with the 6-6 as the pair low hand, and the A-A-A as the three of a kind high hand, you have a dynamite hand in Pai Gow Poker and will win with it most of the time.

• If you have no pairs, no flush, no straight, simply nothing possible out of the seven cards dealt to you, your only choice is to play the highest card you have as the high hand, and the next two highest cards as the low hand. For example, your seven cards are K-Q-10-8-6-4-3, all off-suit. This is a garbage hand. King high is the best this hand will make. In this case you would take the Q-10 as the low hand, and play the remaining five cards, with the king, as the high hand. In this case your hand is called "king high." But this does not mean you will automatically lose. The other advantage of Pai Gow Poker is that *garbage often wins.* Even if such garbage does not win, chances are pretty good you'll make a push out of it. For instance, the banker may only have a J-10 as his highest possible low hand. In this case your Q-10 wins, and it doesn't matter what you have as the high hand. You push, and save yourself from losing the money you bet. In other instances the banker may only have that J-10 up front, and only queen high in the back. Even though you had garbage, your garbage is better than the banker's garbage and you win. Pai Gow Poker is strange this way. No hand, no matter how bad it looks, is an automatic loser, and that's what makes this game exciting, interesting, and often very profitable.

• Take the Bank whenever you can *unless* the dealer, as banker, has been on a run of bad hands (in which case you taking the bank will break the short-term trend and this is not to your advantage) or *unless* the other players at the table offer action too high for your Bankroll. Remember, if you Bank, *you* have to cover *all bets.*

• If you have three pair, which is not unusual in Pai Gow Poker, *always* take the *highest* of the three pairs as the low hand. Remember: *One* pair is lower in value than *two* pairs. If you have, say, K-K, J-J, and 6-6 as the three pairs among your seven cards, place the K-K as the low hand, and keep the two-pair combination of J-J-6-6 as your high hand. *Never* do it the other way around, say, 6-6 or J-J, as in this example. The K-K low hand can *only* be beaten by the banker's K-K or A-A, but if you placed the 6-6 or the J-J as the low hand instead you'd be giving the banker more chances to beat you on the low hand side.

These few suggestions will enable you to approach Pai Gow Poker with enough knowledge to allow for smart decisions. As you play, you will learn other variations and be able to apply your further knowledge, and play experience, to strategy modifications specific to your play at that table at that time. If at any time while you are playing you are not certain of how to play the hand, just ask the dealer. The dealer will tell you how the house would play that hand, and you can then choose whether to play it the safe way, or apply your knowledge to make another choice.

Pai Gow Poker is also a very sociable game. Because it is relatively slow, compared with other casino games, it allows for more camaraderie among players. Personally I find this game quite rewarding from all these perspectives. In addition, the game costs you only the 5 percent house vigorish, and the odds for winning and losing are almost even between players and banker. Banker does have a slight edge, since the banker wins if the banker's hand is *exactly* the same as any player's hand. For example, if you are the banker, and you have, say, 10-10 as your low hand, a terrific high hand, and the house, or any other player betting against you, has the same 10-10 as his low hand, you win. You win because the banker has that edge over players. And since not just the house can be banker, but you can too, it is possible for *you* to get this edge each second turn. So, odds-wise—overall—this game is nearly as good as baccarat, and can be better for the banker.

FORTUNE PAI GOW

Many casinos are now offering a game called "Fortune Pai Gow." This is the standard Pai Gow Poker game with the addition of an optional side bet. Similarly to Progressive Caribbean Stud, this side bet may, or may not, apply to a progressive meter. It depends on the casino, but regardless of whether this is or is not a progressive, the side wager feature can be utilized to good effect and for profit. There are two ways you can win by making this side bet. First, you can be the one whose hand contains the bonus win, in which case you will get paid in accordance with the pay scale (shown opposite). Second, even if you are not the player who hits this bonus hand, you can still win with what's called the "envy bonus." The required minimum bets for this can be as low as $1, but are generally $5 minimum. Again, it depends on the casino that is offering this game, and this version of the bonus.

As with all such "extra" features, be careful not to get too excited, because there is a "cost." The cost here in this bonus is vested in the relatively infrequent occurrence of these hands precisely at the time when you happen to have a bet on the side option in action. This cost is also present in the relatively high house edge on these side bets. Although not nearly as huge as the side bet house edge in games like Progressive Caribbean Stud or Let It Ride, it is still significant, particularly if you are making these side bets as part of your overall playing strategy. If the casino where you are playing allows $1 minimum for this side bet, then the best strategy is to use a figure of 10 percent of the size of your wager as the side bet amount. For a $10 bet, this would be $1, which would be that table's minimum such side bet for this option. For a wager of $20, it would be $2, and so on. However, you should never bet more than $5 on that side option on any event, provided that you are playing this regularly, on each bet. Such extra action will cost you a lot, and I don't recommend it as a viable means to exploit the relatively low average house edge in standard Pai Gow Poker. Perhaps a shot every now and then, but playing these side bets on every hand will cost you too much.

The best and most distinctive feature of this optional side bet is that if any player gets at least a four of a kind, then all other players who placed the side bet get an envy bonus (I guess because they envy the person who got the good hand). The side bet must be at least $5 to qualify for the envy bonus. The return on the side bet is maxed at $5 because the envy bonus is fixed. The winning hand is paid relative to the size of the wager. The following chart shows the winning hands, the number of possible combinations, what it pays to the winner, and the envy bonus. Please note that a straight is more probable than a three of a kind and therefore pays less. A hand that can be arranged to form *both* a three of a kind *and* a straight is calculated as a three of a kind.

Fortune Pai Gow Poker Bonus

HAND	POSSIBLE COMBINATIONS	PAYS	ENVY BONUS
Natural seven-card straight flush	32	8,000 to 1	$5000
Royal flush plus royal match*	72	2,000 to 1	$1000
Wild seven-card straight flush	196	1,000 to 1	$500
Five aces	1,128	400 to 1	$250
Royal flush	26,020	150 to 1	$50
Straight flush	184,644	50 to 1	$20
Four of a kind	307,472	25 to 1	$5
Full house	4,188,528	5 to 1	$0
Flush	6,172,088	4 to 1	$0
Three of a kind	7,521,276	3 to 1	$0
Straight	11,185,428	2 to 1	$0

*A "royal match" is a suited king and queen.

The following chart displays the house edge according to the number of other players at the table making the side bet. The greater the number of other players the greater the probability of an envy bonus and the lesser the house edge. A player making the fortune side bet is eligible for the envy bonus based on the hand of any player, including players not making the fortune side bet themselves. The envy bonus is not payable based on the dealer's hand. The chart is based on the optimal $5 fortune bet size.

Fortune Pai Gow Envy Bonus House Edge

NUMBER OF PLAYERS	HOUSE EDGE (%)
0	7.86
1	6.94
2	6.01
3	5.08
4	4.16
5	3.23

This, then, is all you need to know about Pai Gow Poker, and the Fortune Pai Gow Poker side bet, as they are played in today's casinos. While a whole lot more could be said, it would interest only the very serious players or the analysts. For those of us who are looking for a good, entertaining, and profitable table game, Pai Gow Poker offers yet another opportunity to play well, and learn how to play better. It can be a good game, but as with most casino games, the apparent simplicity of the game belies inherent complexities and well-hidden traps for the unwary. The best advice for playing this game, and for all other casino games, is always to *learn* and *look* before you *leap*.

Three Card Poker

Poker made simple. How easy can it get? Well, how about taking Five-Card Stud, and Seven-Card Stud, and all the hold'em games and reducing the "worry" of what to make out of these cards to just three cards total. Actually, it's quite brilliant. Of course a few rule alterations need to be made. For example, a straight is now higher than a flush. And, there's *no* royal flush—just the straight flush for the top award. The rest of the card hierarchy remains (somewhat) the same: pair, then the flush, then the straight, then the three of a kind and then the straight flush. Of course, there can't be two pairs with just three cards, or a full house or a four of a kind, but then in this game they don't have to be there.

INTRODUCTION TO THREE CARD POKER

The attraction of this game lies in its simplicity, and the "bonus" odds-awards when the higher-paying combinations of cards are hit. Three Card Poker also trades on the familiarity aspects of some other games, which have, by now, become mainstream casino table games. The three games with a familiar presence in Three Card Poker are Stud Poker, Let It Ride, and Caribbean Stud. The brilliance of Three Card Poker lies in how all these three familiar elements have been combined and treated in the game's rules and layout.

The layout of the table is very similar to both Caribbean Stud and Let It Ride. Even the table design, with its three spots, is very like Let It Ride, and the fact that one of the bets is called "ante" and the other called "bet" is also virtually identical to Caribbean Stud. And, of course, stud poker rules are used (somewhat) to judge the value of the hands dealt. So, in one sweep of inspiration, the game's innovator has virtually eliminated the learning curve for players. Anyone who is familiar with stud poker, be it at the poker table or at video poker, knows what the hands do and what they mean. Anyone who has ever played Let It Ride will be able to quickly grasp the layout and betting positions, as will anyone who has ever played Caribbean Stud. Thus, here we have a game that just about anyone who has ever been to a modern casino can play almost immediately, and without much "thinking" and "learning." Three Card Poker is as closely akin to a slot machine as it can possibly be, yet still retain the table game allure both for the players and for the casino.

Three Card Poker is a very good game, odds-wise, for both the player and the casino. The casino can expect an average edge of between 2 percent and 3 percent, while the players can look forward to hitting the top-paying straight flush combination about each 450 hands. All things considered, as far as table games go, this one is among the better-odds games available. Most $1 and $5 and higher slot machines are set to "hold" between 2 percent and 4 percent for the house, and therefore Three Card Poker is very much in line with these house percentages. In addition, the ease of playing the game, and the opportunities to make three bets and vary the betting amounts also provide the player with additional winning opportunities that can't be found among most slot machines, and with an inherent, quite startling simplicity for a table game.

How to Play

After the players make their bets, the game begins by the dealer dealing three cards to each player, and three cards to herself. There are three bets in Three Card Poker. The first is called "pair plus." This is designated on the table layout (closest to the dealer) by a small circle above the ante box. This is a single-shot bet and plays strictly against the pay table. If among your three cards you have at least a pair, you win. Pairs pay even money, three-card flushes pay 4:1, three-card straights pay 6:1, three of a kind pays 30:1, and a three-card straight flush pays 40:1. These are purely one-shot (or one-roll) bets, and the dealer does not figure in this decision. As in Let It Ride, the advantage to the player is that these payoffs pay with substantial odds and are hit more frequently than at other similar games.

The other two bets are the "ante" wager and the "bet" wager. As in Caribbean Stud, the player wagers on the strength and value of his three-card hand against the dealer's three-card hand. The dealer qualifies with a queen or better. If the player's hand beats the dealer, the player wins. If not, the player loses. However, unlike in Caribbean Stud, in Three Card Poker if the player has a hand of straight or better, then the player wins the odds award, regardless of whether the dealer has qualified or not. This is a distinct advantage. Any straight will pay 3:1, a three of a kind pays 4:1, and the straight flush pays 5:1. And all this in addition to the awards paid on these hands for the pair plus wager (if that wager was made by the player).

To sum up, here's how it all works. When you sit down at the Three Card Poker table, and change your cash into gaming chips, you then have the choice of making two of the three bets available: the pair plus and the ante. You *must* make the ante bet if you want to play for the round against the dealer, but otherwise you don't have to, you can simply play pair plus alone. Likewise, you can play only the ante at the beginning, and then decide later if you also want to play the bet round, based on the strength of the cards you received. Let us assume that you are a smart player, and will therefore wager both the pair plus and the ante bets prior to receiving your cards. Now you have two bets in action, and they do *not* have to be the same value bet! This is another advantage, because you can bet, say $25 on the pair plus, and only $5 on the ante. Now that your bets are made, you get your three cards, and the dealer gets his. Look at what you have. If your hand contains a pair or better, you have automatically won your pair plus hand (remember that on the pair plus bet you also are paid for anything better than a pair, such as the flushes, straights, and straight flushes). The pair plus hands are decided first, before the remainder of the game takes place. If your hand won on the pair plus wager, you will be paid in accordance with the pay table. Now the rest of the game takes place.

If you think your hand will beat the dealer's hand, take the third wager in the bet box. (This has to be twice your ante bet, just as in Caribbean Stud.) Then the dealer looks at his hand. If the dealer qualifies with queen or better, whether you win or lose will depend on the value of the dealer's hand versus the value of your hand. If the dealer does not qualify, you will be paid even money on your ante bet. However, if your hand also contains a flush or better, your bet wager will also be paid with odds, regardless of whether or not the dealer qualified. (See the following charts.)

Three Card Poker Hands and Probabilities

HAND	POSSIBILITIES	PROBABILITY (%)
Straight flush	48	00.22
Three of a kind	52	00.24
Straight	720	03.26
Flush	1,096	04.99
Pair	3,744	16,95
Queen to ace high	9,720	43,98
Jack high or less	6,720	30.41

Pay Tables for Pair Plus

HAND	PROBABILITY (%)	TABLE 1	TABLE 2	TABLE 3	TABLE 4
Straight flush	00.22	40 to 1	40 to 1	35 to 1	40 to 1
Three of a kind	00.24	30 to 1	25 to 1	25 to 1	30 to 1
Straight	03.26	6 to 1	6 to 1	6 to 1	6 to 1
Flush	04.96	4 to 1	4 to 1	4 to 1	3 to 1
Pair	16.95	1 to 1	1 to 1	1 to 1	1 to 1
House edge		2.32%	3.49%	4.58%	7.28%

Most casinos used to use only pay table 1, and that is the one upon which I base my strategy recommendations and game analysis. Recently many casinos that play this game—particularly those in gaming jurisdictions outside of Las Vegas—have been reducing the pays on this bonus pay table, and are now using pay table 4. As you can easily see, the house edge in pay table 1 is only 2.32 percent, while using pay table 4 the casinos have increased the house edge to a whopping 7.28 percent. Therefore, be careful when you choose a game, and pay close attention to the pay table.

Compare your casino's pay table with these four, and then you will know exactly how badly the casino wants your money. If they don't offer at least pay tables 1 or 2, don't play this game in that casino.

Ante and Bet Wager Pays

After you have made your ante bet, the rest of the game proceeds as I have explained earlier. Following is the schedule of pays that will be available in most casinos for the ante and bet payoffs.

- If the dealer does *not* qualify, the ante wins 1 to 1, and the bet wager is returned.
- If the dealer *does* qualify, *and* the player's hand beats the dealer, *both* the bet wager and the ante bets win 1 to 1.
- If the dealer qualifies, and the dealer's hand beats the player's hand, then *both* the bet wager and the ante bets *lose.*
- If the dealer qualifies and the dealer's hand *ties* the player's hand, then *both* the bet wager and the ante bets are a push.

There are additional bets and winners that do not depend on the dealer's hand, or on the dealer qualifying, and there are several different pay tables, each with a different house edge. The following chart shows some of the most commonly found pay tables for these ante bet bonuses, along with their house edge and risk factor.

Pay Tables for Ante Bet Bonus

HAND	PROBABILITY (%)	TABLE 1	TABLE 2	TABLE 3	TABLE 4
Straight flush	00.22	5 to 1	4 to 1	3 to 1	5 to 1
Three of a kind	00.24	4 to 1	3 to 1	2 to 1	3 to 1
Straight	03.26	1 to 1	1 to 1	1 to 1	1 to 1
House edge		3.37%	3.83%	4.28%	3.61%
Risk factor		2.01%	2.28%	2.56%	2.16%

Simple Strategy

It's a very good game for the players. Always make the bet wager backing up your ante bet. Most of the time you are far better off doing this than surrendering your ante. In Three Card Poker, your hands will win more than they do at Caribbean Stud, and the fact of the odds payoffs on hands of flush or better regardless of dealer qualifying makes this a very desirable bet. The pair plus is also good, but you should be aware that getting pairs of anything, or better, in Three Card Poker is just about as tough as in five-card based games—in fact tougher. Therefore, the pair plus may not always be a good bet. Nevertheless, the combination of all these three wagers allows you to hedge your total table wagers per round, by cumulative means. This alone is one of the best advantages of this game.

Perhaps the best recommendation for an optimum playing strategy for the ante and bet wagers is to play the bet if you have a queen, with one of the other cards being at least a 6, regardless of the bonus pay table. Playing this way, overall you will lose about 8.7 percent of the original ante bet, but you will win about 5.3 percent on the bonus. So, your overall risk exposure is about 3.4 percent. This is in line with the pair-plus pay table 2, at a 3.49 percent house edge. And that, dear friends, is about all that can be said—simply—about this game.

Caribbean Draw and Super Nines

Iguess it was inevitable that a version of Caribbean Stud that allows players to *draw* replacement cards would eventually find its way to the casino floor. As yet quite rare in most casinos, Caribbean Draw overcomes the major player's complaint about Caribbean Stud: the "draw." As we know, in Caribbean Stud we are stuck with whatever five-card hand we happen to have been dealt, which is why Caribbean Stud is really nothing more than a slot machine played on a table with cards.

CARIBBEAN DRAW

In Caribbean Draw, the players have the choice of asking for up to two replacement cards. This limitation in how many cards players are allowed to draw is a problem, but at least there *is* a draw. The betting is identical to Caribbean Stud: ante plus twice the ante amount as the bet wager. Dealer has to qualify with 8s or better. If she does, then the players are paid based on the value of their hands if they beat the dealer. If the dealer does not qualify, players are paid their ante bets at even money. There is also the $1 progressive jackpot bet, which plays strictly against the pay chart, however only the first initial payer's five cards are considered in action for this side bet (prior to any draw the player may wish to make). Therefore, this side bet is really nothing more than the Caribbean Stud side bet in a new dress.

This game is slow. If you've played Caribbean Stud, you already know how slow that game is, and Caribbean Draw is even slower. It's an "okay" game if you're interested in long hours at the table. Otherwise, it's ho-hum as far as I'm concerned. My recommendation is to never surrender—meaning to *always stay in the hand.* You'll win more often and more when you do.

SUPER NINES

The newest of the table games, Super Nines is not yet widely available. It's basically a fun game, where players don't play against the dealer, but solely against the pay chart. Winning and losing, therefore, depend solely on the kind of cards the players get. There are three bets in action, similar to Let It Ride. However, all three bets must *stay* in action, and therefore the players cannot "take back" two of the three bets, as they can in Let It Ride. The player is first dealt one card, then one more card and then three more cards. The first bet is decided on the one card dealt, as is the second. The third bet is decided based on a five-card poker hand and its relative value based on the pay chart. The second and third bets pay off on hands of pair-twos or higher, and lose otherwise.

The first bet wins or loses depending on whether the player's first card is a 9 or higher. If it is a 9, the player is paid 3:2. If it is higher than a 9, the player is paid even money. If it is neither, the player loses that bet.

The second bet wins or loses depending on whether the two cards the player now has are a pair-twos or higher. However, the second card dealt also pays if it is a 9 or higher, just as the first card dealt for the first wager, in addition to the pays for pair-twos or higher.

The third hand wins or loses depending on the final value of the five-card poker hand. Now it's a stud poker game, with no draw. The players push on pair-twos through pair-eights, and then are paid in progressively higher increments for the remainder of the standard poker-hand hierarchy, all the way up to 1,000-to-one for the royal flush.

It's a simple game, about as simple as table games can get. There are absolutely no player decisions. Players make their bets, and then win or lose depending entirely on what kinds of cards they receive, versus the pay chart. That's it. Therefore, this game is yet another slot machine played on a table with cards. However, it is quite a *good* game, odds-wise.

The overall house edge is a little under 2 percent. On the first and third hands, the house edge is a shade under 4 percent, while on the second bet the *player has an edge over the house* of about 2 percent to 3 percent. This means that the game winds up being fun for both the casino and the player, because, overall, both the casino and its players wind up winning something most of the time. I hope this game will make a bigger impact on the casino floor, since it can be a good distraction from the slots and allows for relaxed camaraderie.

Let It Ride

Let It Ride is a table game manufactured by Shuffle Master, Inc., the company that introduced the Shuffle Master shuffling machines to casinos worldwide. For those of you not familiar with this machine, it is simply a mechanical device that shuffles decks of cards. The machines can now shuffle from one to six decks, and are used in many table games such as blackjack, Let It Ride and Caribbean Stud, as well as in many Pai Gow Poker games. In games like Let It Ride and Caribbean Stud, the machine spits out shuffled hands in preconfigured amounts of cards per player hand.

INTRODUCTION TO LET IT RIDE

The story behind this game is the stuff Hollywood movies are made of. As the myth goes, this tale of success began one rainy day in a truck stop somewhere on the long-haul truck routes in the midwestern United States. A trucker from Minnesota, by the name of John Breeding, was mulling over an article he read in the *Wall Street Journal*—at least that's what it says in the Shuffle Master PR kit (it should already be obvious that John Breeding was no ordinary truck driver, since he was reading the *Wall Street Journal* rather than some of the other, more popular, men's publications). Anyhow—so the story goes—this particular article was about the problems many Atlantic City casinos were having with card counters at their blackjack tables. A card counter is a professional blackjack player who has mastered a system of tracking the cards, and thus is able to beat the game in most sessions. This is not illegal, but casinos don't like card counters because they win so much. This fateful truck stop and cogitation took place in 1982. John Breeding became convinced that he could invent a machine that would shuffle cards. Such a machine, he thought, would provide more random shuffles and eliminate "clumping," dealer cheating, and other such "human" situations, and therefore would be very desirable for the casinos. So, he set out to invent one. It took him ten years, but by 1992, he succeeded and his company—Shuffle Master, Inc.—launched their first series of card-shuffling machines. At that stage, these machines could only shuffle one deck at a time. This wasn't very useful for most of the casinos, since by that time casino blackjack games—for which this shuffling machine was originally designed—were played with two-deck or multi-deck shoes. So, John had to do a little more thinking, and invented Let It Ride.

Let It Ride is ideally suited to the single-deck shuffling machine, and by inventing it, John Breeding also invented the market for his machine. Not only did he now have a new game he could sell, but one specifically designed to use his shuffling machine. And so the legend was born. By 1993, the Let It Ride game was launched. It quickly became a huge hit, and the rest—as they say—is history.

The Game

Let It Ride uses John Breeding's shuffling machines to distribute players' hands around the table. Although initially only played in Nevada casinos, the game has now become available everywhere. Let It Ride may look perplexing when you first walk up to the table, but it's a very simple game—one that employs very few player decisions. It is a poker-style game, similar to draw poker in that the game uses only five cards total. It is also similar to Texas Hold'Em poker, since two of the cards are common cards to all the players at the table (the dealer's two cards). In some respects, it also mirrors Caribbean Stud, but the similarity is only marginal. In Let It Ride, however, the players *do not* play against the dealer, since the dealer's cards are common cards to *all* players. Therefore, your action is solely against the house, based on the cards drawn and nothing else. Let It Ride is played on a blackjack-size table with, traditionally, six player positions. Each player position is clearly defined on the table and includes a description of the various payoffs on winning hands and three betting circles (or betting areas). For those games that also employ the bonuses there is also a large red spot in front of each player position which lights up when a silver dollar is placed over it. This signifies that this player has entered the bonus option (more on this a little later).

How to Begin

As with all table games, you begin by exchanging your cash for gaming chips when you first sit down. Most Let It Ride games have a table limit of a minimum of $5 per bet and a maximum of $50 per bet, though these amounts vary from casino to casino. Let It Ride uses a single deck of cards, no joker and no wild cards. Two decks are commonly used in the game: one which is currently used for the hand in progress and the other being shuffled by the machine so that it will be ready for the next hand. These decks are exchanged in this manner, the idea being that the game will flow faster with one deck always ready for the hand in progress and the other being shuffled in the meantime. The betting areas are divided into three circular "spots." To be in the game, you *must* make a bet in *each of the three areas,* and these bets *must be of equal value.* For example, $5 in the first spot, $5 in the second spot, and $5 in the third spot—a total of $15. This may sound like a lot to bet, but you are only risking the third $5 spot bet. In Let It Ride, you have the option of pulling back your first two bets, once in each round of dealing during the current hand, depending on whether or not you want to "let it ride."

How It Works

Assuming that you are betting the minimum table requirement (in this example I will use $5 as that minimum), you place your $5 chips into the three circular spots in the betting area of the table layout directly in front of where you are sitting. By this time the shuffling machine has already shuffled the deck, and the game is ready to begin. When all players at the table have made their bets, the dealer pushes a button on the shuffling machine and the machine proceeds to spit out player hands. Each player hand consists of three cards. The dealer picks up the cards from the machine and spreads them face down in front of each player position. The last hand out of the machine is the dealer's hand. The dealer places the topmost card in the dealer's card box 1, the next card in the dealer's card box 2. The third card, the bottom card from that set of dealer's three cards, then becomes the burn card and is placed by the dealer into the discard tray.

Depending on the casino rules where you are playing, you may either look at your hand immediately after you have received it, or you may have to wait until player hands have been distributed to each player at the table. When all hands, including the dealer's hand, have been properly distributed, the dealer presses the machine's button again and the machine spits out the rest of the unused cards. The dealer then places the remainder of this deck into the discard tray, and the game is ready to continue. Once you have received your cards, you look at the three cards in your hand. At this stage, *both* dealer's cards are *face down.* If your three-card hand already constitutes a winner, or if you think it may make a winner during the next two rounds, you can choose to stay. You indicate this either by waving your hand slightly (as in blackjack) indicating "stay," or, which is more accurate, you stack your cards together and gently place them face down under the *middle* bet. If you *do not wish to continue* with this current *first bet,* you "scratch" your cards on the table (like in blackjack, where this motion would indicate you want a "hit"), in which case in Let It Ride the dealer will push back to you the *first* bet in that first bet betting circle. This goes on for each player at the table. Once all players have made their decisions in this "first round" of the current hand in progress, the dealer turns one of the dealer's cards face up (the one to dealer's left, player's right in the dealer's card box areas). Remember, that *both dealer's cards count as all players' cards,* so you can use both of these dealer's cards as part of *your* hand. If, on the dealer's first turn, your hand has improved to an immediate winner, or you think that it may do so on the last turn, you can then stack your cards and place them face down under the *third* circle betting area wager. If, however, you *do not* want to "let it ride," you can again repeat the "scratch" procedure, and the dealer will *return your second bet* back to you. At this point you have no further options, and you *must* place your cards under the *third* circled betting area wager. That bet then rides for the final decision. This entire procedure is repeated for all players at the table. The final, and *third stage,* involves the dealer turning over the dealer's *second down card* (the dealer's second, and final, turn). Again, *this card is also common to all players at the table.* Therefore, in the end, each player has three cards in hand (actually tucked under the third bet), and two common cards (the dealer's two cards), thus making each player's hand a total of five cards.

What Wins, How and How Much

Whether you win or lose depends entirely on which cards you are given at the *first round,* and which hand you ultimately make out of your set of three cards *combined with* the dealer's two cards. Poker rules are used. There is *no draw*—meaning you cannot ask for any more cards, or ask to have your cards replaced (as you may do in standard draw poker games). Consequently, Let It Ride is basically a slot machine game played on a live-game table, with cards instead of slot machine symbols. You, as the player, have *no control* over how your hand comes out in the end. Players' decisions are based solely on a hierarchy of possible winning hands. The payoff chart is as follows:

HAND	PAYS
Royal flush	1,000-to-1
Straight flush	200-to-1
Four of a kind	50-to-1
Full house	11-to-1
Flush	8-to-1

HAND	PAYS
Straight	5-to-1
Three of a kind	3-to-1
Two pairs	2-to-1
Pair of 10s or better	1-to-1

Advantages

Unlike most video poker machines whereby the poker game pays even money for pairs of jacks or better, Let It Ride pays even money for pairs of *10s or better.* This is also somewhat better than Caribbean Stud, since in Let It Ride the dealer does not have to "qualify" before making payoffs. Another advantage is that you can make *three bets,* but *risk only one*—because you have the option of "taking back" the first two bets. The biggest advantage in Let It Ride is if you receive a "pat hand" from the start. By that I mean a hand that is already a winner—such as a pair of 10s, jacks, queens, kings, or aces, or any three of a kind—even before the dealer's two cards are turned over. Any of these hands showing up among your *first three cards* means that *you have won already,* regardless of what the two common cards are (which the dealer turns up). You should therefore stay in all rounds, knowing that you *cannot lose* and can *only improve* your hand from that point on.

Another advantage is in situations wherein the dealer turns up a pair of 10s or better. Since the dealer's cards are common cards to all players, if this happens *all players win,* regardless of what they have as their three cards. The problem with this situation is that if you had a lousy hand to start with, and did not improve it when the first dealer's card was turned up, by the time you find out that the dealer's cards made a "pat hand" for all the players at the table, including yourself, you would have ordinarily already taken back your first two bets and therefore will only have the last bet "in play" (which you cannot take back). But the up side is that you have a winner, and got one even though your initial three cards were trash. Since you cannot take back your last (third) bet, these situations work in your favor by providing you with a winner that you would not have ordinarily received. This is better than blackjack, where if you surrender you lose half of your bet. Situations such as these—whereby the dealer's two cards count as a winner for everyone in the game—are rare. Nevertheless, this is an advantage, particularly if you already have another pair or three of a kind, and thus the fact that the dealer turned up a paying pair will provide you with an even bigger win—two pairs or full house, for example.

Disadvantages

There is *no draw* in Let It Ride, which means that *you cannot make any decisions concerning the ultimate outcome of your hand.* Also, if you have marginal hands, such as a flush draw, or a straight draw, or a pair of 9s or less, you then stand the risk of "letting it rido" and potentially losing much more than just your base required minimum bet. That's the catch in this game, and that's primarily why the game generally has a large house edge.

Bonus Pays

In those casinos that offer the bonus pay versions of Let It Ride, the game also employs a large red circle, which lights up when you place a silver dollar over it (or one of the $1 tokens, which are now generally used instead of actual silver dollars). Betting this extra dollar in this area allows the player to participate in the various bonuses being offered by the bonus payoff hierarchy. If you bet that extra dollar, and if you get one of the following hands, you will be paid *extra* bonus pays, as follows:

HAND	PAYS
Royal flush	Bonus of $20,000
Straight flush	Bonus of $2,000
Four of a kind	Bonus of $200
Full house	Bonus of $75
Flush	Bonus of $50
Straight	Bonus of $20

These are bonus pays, paid *in addition* to whatever you will win based on the bets you have in the game to the final stage of the hand in progress. This particular pay table came from a game I played at Caesars Palace and the Mirage, in Las Vegas. As you will see from the bonus pay table chart (page 176), there are now about eight different pay tables in play at various casinos. These are more recent modifications, and are therefore the kinds of pay tables you are now more likely to find.

House Edge for Standard Let It Ride

There are 311,875,200 ways to choose five cards out of fifty-two, with regard to the order chosen. The total amount the player would lose, assuming perfect strategy, over all possible combinations, is 10,933,344. The house edge is defined as the average player loss to the minimum bet, which it turns out is about 3.51 percent.

House Edge on the Bonus Side Bet

In those casinos that play the side bet of $1, you will receive additional payoffs with certain paying hands, as I have shown above. The house edge varies from 13.77 percent to

Pay Table (PT) Chart for the Let It Ride Bonus Side Bet

HAND	PT 1	PT 2	PT 3	PT 4	PT 5	PT 6	PT 7	PT 8
Royal flush	20,000	20,000	20,000	20,000	20,000	10,000	20,000	20,000
Straight flush	2,000	1,000	2,000	2,000	1,000	2,000	2,000	1,000
Four of a kind	100	100	100	400	400	100	300	300
Full house	75	75	75	200	200	75	150	150
Flush	50	50	50	50	50	50	50	50
Straight	25	25	25	25	25	25	25	25
Three of a kind	9	4	8	5	5	8	5	5
Two pairs	6	3	4	0	0	4	0	0
High pair	0	1	0	0	0	0	0	0

Note: These are the pay tables for the Bonus Pays of Let It Ride that you are likely to find in various casinos. (This chart refers to information on page 175.)

36.52 percent. The chart opposite shows some payoff tables at several popular casinos (mostly in Las Vegas), and their house edge—shown in order left-to-right from best to worst (PT means "pay table," and the number behind it means which of the eight casino pay tables this is—PT 1 means pay table 1 at the best casino, and so on).

Where to Play

Based on the pay tables for the side bet, the casinos where you should play—as well as those you should avoid as your choice for Let It Ride—are as follows:

- Table 1: Lady Luck, Las Vegas
- Table 2: Las Vegas Club, Freemont, Californian, Plaza, Main Street Station, Bally's, Circus Circus, Hilton—all in Las Vegas, plus: Grand (Biloxi), Beau Rivage (Biloxi), Horseshoe (Tunica), Grand (Tunica)
- Table 3: Golden Gate, Las Vegas
- Table 4: Bellagio, Excalibur, Mandalay Bay, Harrah's, Imperial Palace, Paris, Venetian—all in Las Vegas
- Table 5: MGM Grand and Golden Nugget, in Las Vegas
- Table 6: Colorado Belle (Laughlin), Sky City (Acoma, New Mexico)
- Table 7: Four Queens and the Flamingo Hilton, in Las Vegas
- Table 8: New York New York, in Las Vegas (the worst place to play Let It Ride)

Remember that these recommendations are based only on the bonus side bet. The house edge for the main standard game remains at the steady 3.51 percent, because Let It Ride is an *independent* game, just like roulette: once the shuffle has taken place, the order of the cards is predetermined for that hand, and all player spots at the table will get those cards, and those cards only, for the duration of that one deal. Unlike in blackjack, for example, where those cards that have already been dealt out have a direct impact on those cards that are still left to be dealt—thus making blackjack a *dependent* game—in Let It Ride, and other such independent-event games, nothing that happens after this one deal has any mathematical bearing on what comes on the next deal. This is the same as the spin on a slot machine, the deal in video poker, the spin of the roulette wheel, or the toss of the dice in Craps. Therefore, the only real method of choosing which is the better game is to look for the bonus pay tables, as shown in the charts. This will show you to what extent the casino wants to take your money, and how fast.

As a general rule of thumb, the worse the pay table is for the bonus bets, the worse the game is likely to be in that casino. Most of the time, if you find that the casino falls into the really bad category for these bonus side bet pays, it is usually a good indication that the rest of the game's pay table may also be somewhat altered, and not necessarily for the better as far as you, the player, are concerned. This is also a good indication that this casino's other games may not be as good as those you could find elsewhere, so take a close look at the pays and payoffs on the other table games as well. While this is not always so—since many casinos may offer the worst bonus pay table but a much better one elsewhere in the main game—it is usually a good gauge by which you can generally get a quick feel of just where this casino may stand on offering the better paying table games and their various options. As I've said many times, it pays to be aware, and it pays to take a few minutes to look and snoop around. What you find and discover may save you a lot of money, and will make it far more possible for you to make powerful profits from all of your gaming.

Simple Strategy

Let It Ride is a notoriously streaky game. Basically, just like slots. When you are getting good hands, you will win regularly. When you are not, there's nothing you can do about it (other than leave the game). There are virtually no player decisions involved, and this inherent simplicity is what has made the game so popular. There are, however, some recommendations which I can make.

- If you wish to win at Let It Ride, start with only the *minimum* bet requirement. Increase the amount of your bet only if you are winning substantially, and even then think twice about it. In this game you can lose very quickly, so don't risk too much unless you're ahead of the game by at least 100 percent above your initial starting buy-in amount.
- *Always* take back your first bet, *unless* you have a "pat hand" (a *paying* hand) from the start.
- *Always* take back your second bet, *unless* you have made a paying hand after the dealer turned up the first of the two dealer's cards (which are common to everyone in the game, including you).
- *Don't* "let it ride" if you have only a marginal "maybe" chance, such as a small pair (9s or less), or a flush or straight draw. Most of the time you will wind up losing if you "let it ride," and therefore these situations are substantially a sucker bet.
- If you have a pair of 10s or better, you have a "pat hand" and therefore *always stay in for ALL rounds of that hand.* You have already won!
- Let the *first* bet ride *only* if you have a draw to a straight flush or a royal flush. Don't do it otherwise, or it will cost you. If you *do not improve* your hand on the second round, pull back your second bet. That

way you have only the first and third bets riding, and *only* in these straight flush or royal flush situations.

- Don't be upset if you make a hand on the last turn and you didn't stay in for the first- and second-round bets. It's better to win something than risk losing it all. And even a small win at Let It Ride, with only the last bet still in "action," can be substantial.

- Many people will habitually "let it ride" from the start, sometimes not even looking at the cards they get. This is silly and expensive. Regardless of what you see other players do at the table, and regardless of what you *think* you can make out of the three-card hand you first receive, *don't let other players' bad play influence you*. It's your money, so *play to win* and *not to lose*.

- Your best chance at winning is to *improve* a pat hand, and *not* trying to win a marginal hand. If you take the first bet down, and on the first dealer's turn you see that you have made a winning hand, you still have two bets that *win*. Don't risk your money unless you know for sure you have a winning hand. I was dealt two queens once, and the dealer turned up the other two queens. I *improved my original pat hand* and made a four of a kind for $750, and did so without having my bets at risk, since I already had a pat hand to start with. And that's the only way you'll have consistent wins at this game.

- Probably the best strategy advice I can give you is *seat selection*. Let It Ride, and Caribbean Stud, *always* deal cards left-to-right of the dealer's position (right-to-left from the player's view). Therefore, *first base* will *always* get the first hand out, while *every other hand will change as players come in and out of the game*. Consequently, if you are sitting at the first-base position and you are getting good cards, this will not change because the player in front of you has left or has come into the game. You will always be the first to get cards; this is very powerful in this game. In any other seat on the table, your order of cards will alter as players leave and come in. If you are sitting elsewhere at the table and happen to be receiving consistently (or reasonably so) good hands, and the player in front of you in the dealing process is getting terrible hands, and that player leaves, *you* will now be getting that player's bad hands and the player behind you, in turn of dealing, will be getting *your* good hands. Consequently, it's better to sit at the one table position where nothing like this can happen, and where your cards will not change because of other players' movements in and out of the game. Of course, this doesn't mean that you will be getting consistently good hands—you may be getting dogs, but at least you won't be victim to other players' fluctuations.

Additional Strategy Suggestions

There are several other strategy notes that could be included, many of which are dependent on the various rule alterations found in some casinos. For example, several casinos have aggregate limits to the top jackpot pays. So, while the top jackpot is the royal flush, and even though it may say that such pays 1,000-to-1, there may also be a smaller note, printed somewhere on the table layout or on the table pay scale and table limits sign, that says something like this: "Table limited to $50,000 aggregate." What this means is that if you bet $50 and hit the royal flush, your 1,000-to-1 pay should be $50,000, but because it is a table maximum aggregate of $50,000, your award will now be reduced by the amount of the pays that are awarded to other players in that same hand.

But that's not the worst of it—what if you wagered $100? Well, according to the 1,000-to-1 payoff, you should have been paid $100,000 for that win. Right? Wrong! On tables that show such a stated aggregate limit, this means that no matter how much you bet, your win will always be limited only to that aggregate. So, in the above example, instead of being paid $100,000 for that win, you will only be entitled to $50,000, and this will be further eroded by other wins at the table at the same time you hit your big winner. This is important to remember if you are playing at these stakes, and many people do play $25, and $50, and more per spot.

For additional strategy recommendations, I offer the following:

- Never bet more than the table's aggregate limit allows for the top award jackpot, or any of the stated pays. Carefully check to see if this table has such a stated aggregate, and if it does, what it is. If the table lists *any* aggregate, *limit your bet to the proportional size.* For example, if your table lists a $25,000 maximum aggregate, then never bet more than $25 in any hand. If the aggregate is at $50,000, never bet more that $50 per in any hand, and so on.
- With *three* cards in hand, "let it ride" only if you have:
  - Any paying hand (10s or better, three of a kind)
  - Any three to a royal flush
  - Three suited cards in a row except 2-3-4, and ace-2-3
  - Three to a straight flush with at least one high card (10 or greater)
  - Three to a straight flush with at least two high cards
- With *four* cards—after the dealer has turned over his first hole card, thus making your hand into four cards at this stage—"let it ride" *only* if you have:

- Any paying hand (10s or better, two pairs, three of a kind)
- Any four to a royal flush
- Any four to a straight flush
- Any four to a flush
- Any four to an open-ended straight with at least one high card
- Any four to an open-ended straight with no high cards
- Any four to an inside straight with four high cards

Well, that's about it for Let It Ride. As I said, it's a simple game, but it takes time, patience, and a good bankroll to sustain play at it. Most of the time you will *not* get "pat" hands to start with, and therefore if you don't play smart you can lose a lot very fast. But, you can also win quickly, and that's where the key decisions I have listed come into play.

VIDEO LET IT RIDE

This video version mimics the table game. It is basically configured as a video poker machine, and can be found either as a stand-alone self-contained machine or as part of some multi-game video slots. Some of the video Let It Ride machines are also made very big—meaning that their video screens, and the cabinets the machines are contained in, are large. It doesn't matter whether the game is in a small cabinet, or whether it is one of the big machines, or whether the game is simply part of the game icons in a multi-game machine. All versions of video Let It Ride play the same.

Video Let It Ride is a player-interactive game similar to video poker. You play it in virtually the same manner as you would *any* video poker machine. The only major difference in operating video Let It Ride, as opposed to video poker machines, is that there are fewer buttons. The buttons on this game, which control your decisions, are: "bet one," "bet max," "rebet," "help," "credits," and "cash out." In addition, video Let It Ride has two other buttons that tell the machine whether you wish to "take down" the first or second hand bet. After you deposit the number of coins you wish to bet—on these machines from one to five for each spot—and after the machine deals you the three cards you get to see first, it will then prompt you to decide whether or not you wish to "let it ride." Press the button marked "yes" or "no." The machine does it all.

Playing this game is virtually the same as playing the table version of Let It Ride. The only difference is that this is a machine, and therefore the action is only between you and it. That can be an advantage. The disadvantage, however, is that you can *only* bet a maximum of $5 per spot—on a $1 machine—and thus are limited in your betting choices. Also, video Let It Ride only offers fixed payoffs, and these are pretty small when compared with what you can get on the table game version, particularly with the various payoff variations and bonus games offered by some (but not all) casinos for the table-game version. Although video Let It Ride can be fun to play for a tryout, you're far better off playing the table-game version, where you can control the size of your bets and have the ability to choose tables and seating positions, as well as seeing the flow of cards dealt to other players. This video version of Let It Ride can also get quite boring after a while, and it is therefore not recommended as one of the better video slot machines. If you are interested in more information about the kinds of slots, or video poker machines and games that I do recommend, please look them up in my books on slots and video poker.

Casino War

Idecided to include this short chapter on Casino War because this game has gained a far greater popularity in recent times than it ever before enjoyed. You are quite likely to find this game on the main casino floor, usually in the main pit, and most major casinos will have at least one table open at all times. To my mind, it is a very silly game, one that wastes both time and money. Nevertheless, many people play it, and many of them don't even know—or realize—just how bad it is. For these reasons, I have decided to break down the game for you so that you can make up your own mind and, I hope, learn to stay away from it.

INTRODUCTION TO CASINO WAR

Casino War is without a doubt the easiest card game to play in the casino. If you have ever played War as a kid, or simply made a bet on who could draw the highest card, then Casino War should look instantly familiar.

How to Play and Game Rules

The game is usually played with six decks. Cards are ranked by the traditional poker hierarchy, except that aces are always high. The suits don't matter and do not figure in the game. After the players have made a bet, each player and the dealer gets one card. Each player's card is compared with the dealer's card. If the player's card is higher, he wins even money. If the dealer's card is higher, the player loses. In the event of a tie the player has two choices:

- Surrender and forfeit half the bet
- Go to war

If the player elects to go to war he must raise his bet by an amount equal to his original wager. The dealer will do the same, but this is just for show. The dealer will then burn three cards and give the player and dealer another card each. If the player's second card equals or beats the dealer, the player wins even money on the raise only, and the original wager will push. If the dealer's second card is greater than the player's, the player loses *both* bets. At some casinos—such as the Mirage in Las Vegas—a tie *after* a tie will result in a bonus equal to the original wager. Normally, the casino will say that the raise pays 3-to-1, but the initial bet loses, which is mathematically the same thing. A tie bet is also available, which pays 10-to-1 if the first two cards tie.

House Edge

Under normal rules, when the player does not get a bonus on a tie after a tie, the house edge is 2.88 percent. Under the bonus rules, the house edge is 2.33 percent. If the player forfeits on ties, the house edge is 3.70 percent. The house edge on the tie bet is 18.65 percent (Craps propositions, any-one?).

House edge with more decks

Some casinos will use fewer decks, and some even only one deck (usually online casinos). The following chart shows the house edge according to various numbers of decks, under the non-bonus rules.

Casino War House Edge

NUMBER OF DECKS	HOUSE EDGE (%)
1	2.42
2	2.70
4	2.84
6	2.88
8	2.90

Is there a simple strategy for this game? Well, yes, there is—don't play it! This has to be the silliest game ever to make its way to the casino table games pit area. Watching paint dry or grass grow is far more exciting, and profitable. My advice is to take a look at it if you must, then just keep on walking. It will be a lot more profitable for you to select some of the other games, which are not only more fun, but usually also better paying.

Keys to Winning

If you have read any of my other books, you will be familiar with the material in this chapter. Some of this information is universal—meaning it applies to all gambling games. However, there are also other points that apply only to the games under discussion. If you are a first-time reader of my books, all of this will be new.

In writing a series of gambling books it's often difficult to strike a balance between information that should be shared, and the problem of repeating information already given in other books. I struggle to make this material fresh, yet complete for those readers who may be reading it for the first time by *focusing* each item of knowledge in my Keys To Winning chapters on how these keys apply to the *specific games* we are discussing, yet indicating wherever possible that these principles can be applied to all other casino games, and indeed to all of your casino gambling. Your ability to win on these casino games is not only limited to acquiring the knowledge of the games, and the skills of playing them, but also depends on how well you prepare yourself to deal with these experiences as a whole.

It's not easy. Simplicity belies complexity. Most of the casino games I have discussed in this book are not just the simple, dumb games that most people think they are. They are all serious gambling games, most of which have a high house withholding percentage. These games can—and will—take your money fast if you don't know how to make winning at them work for you. Similarly, it becomes increasingly necessary for you to gain sufficient mastery of these key concepts to overcome the misinformation available in many forms, and particularly that as presented in the casino's guides to playing, brochures, and rate card examples. To learn this takes time, and the willingness not just to learn it, but also to apply the knowledge and skills, and apply them correctly. To help you do this, I have created the Keys to Winning. These are, in order of importance as I see them, as follows:

- Knowledge
- Patience
- Bankroll
- Selection
- Discipline
- Win goal

Simple, right? No problem. I can do that. Can you? Really? Be honest, now. I can tell you from direct personal experience that sticking to these principles is extremely hard to do. To be a successful player, and win most of the time, you *must* keep to these principles. If you leave home to go to a casino, and you leave just one of these principles behind, you're sunk. You're the *Titanic* on a collision course with the iceberg, and there's no stopping the final result, or the consequences. And that's no joke. Believe me. I know. I am a human being. Nobody can be perfect at all times, and I don't expect you to be either. Just *most of the time,* that's all we can ask of each other. There will be times when you will have the best intentions, but you will fail. You will leave home without one, or more, of these vital principles. And you will regret it.

We are frail creatures, mentally, physically and, most important, emotionally. We get upset. We get angry. We get mad that we have done everything perfectly, and still we lost. It happens. That's also part of life, and certainly part of the gaming experience. Even when you take all these principles with you, and do everything perfectly, there will be times when you will lose. This I also know from personal experience. There are statistical anomalies that infect every aspect of gambling, and the games in this book are among the most prone to such visible fluctuations.

My aim here is to help you *become more secure in your gaming,* more steady in your approach, more confident in your end result, and more conscious of your expectations. These are the real secrets to your success playing these games. So, let's address each of these key principles individually.

KNOWLEDGE

This should be relatively easy. This is the "learning curve," the decision to improve yourself, and probably the reason you bought this book. Knowledge means to learn as much as possible, with as good a direction toward your end goal as possible. Knowledge means to know not just that these games exist, but also how to play them *well.* Playing these games *well* also means incorporating into your knowledge all the other principles of these Keys to Winning. Knowledge is growth in understanding and in continual improvement. Learning will have a direct and positive impact on your play, and on your life, and specifically on how you approach the game the very next time you visit a casino.

PATIENCE

I am often surprised at how easily people get upset. They get upset when they don't win. They get upset when they do win, but they don't think it's enough. They get upset if they don't hit the jackpot. When they hit a secondary jackpot, they get upset that they didn't hit the top jackpot. And when they hit the top jackpot, unless it's something in the millions, they get upset as to why they couldn't hit it sooner. Are you this kind of a player? Does this fit your playing profile? If it does, then you aren't patient. You are hyper. You shouldn't play these games, at least not without a tranquilizer. Playing these games can be a very prolonged experience, one which will require your utmost patience. Wins will happen, and although sometimes you may be lucky and get that good win right away, most of the time it will not come that easy. You will have to work for it for a while. This may require you to do several sessions, and perhaps even visit several casinos. Maybe you will have to make several trips before you achieve that desired win goal. Setting achievable win goals is part of the art of patience.

I call it the "art" of patience because that's what it is. Patience is not a skill, and it is not science. It is art. Skills can be learned. Science can be learned. But you are born with the *ability* to be patient. Unfortunately, the pace of our modern world rarely rewards patience, at least visibly. Although most achievements that we see publicly are the result of hard work and a lot of patience, when we see these achievements they have already happened. To us, these seem to have happened overnight. Such examples are here to demonstrate that success playing these games is not merely that once-in-a-lifetime blind luck event. You can be successful as a player each time you play, overall throughout your career, but only if you develop your art of patience. Notice I said *develop,* rather than acquire. Like the ability to draw, you must practice and learn, and learn from doing, and learn from mistakes. It won't be easy, but then nothing worthwhile usually is. Developing patience means that you will curb your natural reactions, the emotional bursts, such as exuberance when you win, and anger when you lose.

First, the trick to developing the art of patience is to realize that great and glorious wins *will* happen. Also, to realize that equally great and horrendous *losses* will also happen. Both are the extremes among life's probabilities. Second, learn to develop your ability to curb your reactions to those extremes. Be happy when you win, but remember that this is not an event that will always happen like this. Don't start expecting this will always happen. Remember that the money you *don't* lose back today will spend very nicely tomorrow, with a cooler head and a clearer perspective. When you lose, curb your reaction equally. Don't start to question yourself beyond reason. If you feel you have forgotten some part of your knowledge, look it up. See if you were correct, and if so, learn from the experience. When you realize that you did everything correctly, and still suffered that great and horrendous loss, curb your instinct to blame everything and everybody, and try not to destroy yourself or the solid foundations of your playing abilities. Remember that the pendulum of overall probability simply swung against you. It will swing back. That's the reality, and it will always happen like that. It may take what you consider a long time.

What you may consider as "a long time" may in reality

only be a tiny fraction of a micro-second in the overall scope of universal time. It's all relative. If you play a game for two hours and don't reach your win goal, was that losing streak "a long time"? Well, for you, perhaps. But you should be conscious of the fact that the universe doesn't revolve around your particular perception of reality, or length of time. Patience, therefore, is the art of being able to react to each situation *without overreacting to it.* You will have to work this out yourself, because no two people deal with the same set of circumstances in exactly the same way. No specific advice is possible. However, a plausible *guideline* to achieving patience *is* possible, and that's why this section of this chapter explores the art of patience in such detail. Patience will not only enable you to play better, but will also allow you to reach your comfort level far quicker and with far more positive results. By realizing that patience is a requirement for enjoyment, and profit, from your play, you will become far more at ease with the process. This will relax you under a variety of circumstances and situations, and will in turn allow you to take a far more rational, and less emotional, approach to whatever these situations may bring.

BANKROLL

All of these Keys to Winning are important, but bankroll is perhaps the foremost. The reason is quite simple: without money, you can't gamble. Gambling is all about money— losing it and, of course, winning. You must have it to start. You can't start without it. Even credit is money, and so is a credit line at the casino. It doesn't matter how you acquire your money, but whatever money you bring with you, send to the casino cage, or get in credit at the casino, constitutes your bankroll. This is the money you have designated as your gambling money. Your gambling stake. It should not be money you need for your family's rent, mortgage, food, clothing, health care, and so on. This should be accumulated "spare" money, something you can afford to lose without such a loss having a devastating impact on you and your family. Any gambling bankroll should be made up of money that you have designated as *expendable.* This doesn't mean that it should be treated as already lost, and hence treated recklessly. After all, it's still your money. You may have worked for it for a year, or more, and saved it up for your casino trip. You may have accumulated it through interest on investments, or from the sale of something you made or sold, and you don't need the money for your survival. Remember that it is still your money, and even though it should be considered expendable, this is still important money and should be highly regarded. It was your work that made it possible. Just because you designate it as your gambling money, doesn't mean it has suddenly lost its value. It still spends just the same.

Many people make the classic mistake of setting aside their gambling money with the conviction that it's already gone, dead, done, lost, and therefore it means nothing. Wrong! This is a defeatist attitude, and it has no business in your psychological makeup. Thinking like this will result in two inevitable occurrences.

First, you have already convinced yourself that you are a loser, that you will lose, and therefore this money is already lost, so, you will gamble recklessly, without regard to the value of the money or the consequences of your reckless actions. You will lose, and this will reinforce your conviction that "Ah, well, it was already lost. I knew it." So, you will be happy in your loss, because you convinced yourself that it was inevitable.

Second, you will not play knowledgeably, and certainly

not in concert with these Keys to Winning. So, again, you will lose. When you do, this becomes yet another reinforcement of your initial starting attitude. "So," you now say to yourself, and quite possibly to anyone who will listen, "it was only gambling money. I knew I was gonna lose it, so what? It was my 'mad' money anyway. Ah, well. Maybe next time." You have now thoroughly convinced yourself that you are a loser, and you have justified your initial defeatist attitude by making sure that you lost.

Your bankroll is your gambling lifeline. It is essential and should be treated valuably, protected, and handled with care. In addition, it must be sufficient to carry the weight of your action. How much is in this bankroll should be determined by a couple of factors. First, it depends on what this money means to you at that time. If this money is truly unencumbered, you will feel a lot better about making it a true bankroll. If this money is *not* completely unencumbered, such as when a portion of it should be used for something else, you will not handle the bankroll as well, or it may not be big enough. As a general rule, any gambling bankroll should be made up only of entirely unencumbered money, with no part of it needed for something else. Unencumbered money is free, and not scared. Encumbered money will always be scared money, and in gambling, scared money will quickly fly away. Playing with scared money means you are afraid to lose it. This doesn't mean that you have adopted the defeatist attitude discussed earlier. This simply means that you have allocated at least some part of your bankroll either as an inadequate amount, or encumbered upon something else—borrowed from a credit card maybe—which means you will have to pay it back, and probably have to do so at great stress to you, or your family. This is a bad way to start your bankroll. Always start your bankroll with free money, which will become a solid gambling stake and not frightened at the prospect of being lost.

Second, the amount of your bankroll should be determined by the kind of game you intend to play. If you wish to play $75 per bet in these games, your bankroll should reflect that action. If you wish to play higher limits than that, your bankroll should be equally higher. If you plan to play only $1 per hand, your bankroll should adjust to that. In addition, whatever your action, or intended action, your bankroll should be adequate to withstand fluctuations, not only in your fortunes as you play, but also in your decisions concerning the *kinds* of games you will play. For example, you may have decided to play $1 roulette on this trip, and allocated your bankroll for that action. But when you get to the casino, you discover that the game you wanted to play has been changed: payoffs have been reduced, the game is gone, or any number of factors that work against your pre-designed plan. Now what? Your bankroll should have a "slush" factor, allowing it to withstand the necessity for such on-the-spot decisions. What if you saw another kind of game, perhaps a game in a different casino and with different payoffs? Your bankroll should be adaptable to such deviations from your initial starting strategy and your perception of what your action will be.

How do you arrive at the bankroll figure? Hard to say. It's all individual to each player, and to you. You know yourself, and your circumstances. All *I* can do is offer you *guidelines,* with the hope that you will have learned enough in this book to intelligently adapt this guideline to your specific situation.

If you plan to play about four hours per day, for an average of three days, consider the following chart for your guideline:

Recommended Minimum Bankroll

Baccarat ($25 table)	$2,500
Baccarat ($10 table)	$1,000
Mini-Baccarat ($5 table)	$500
Roulette ($1 chips, $5 spread)	$800
Roulette (50 cents, $2.50 spread)	$350
Roulette (25 cents, $1 spread)	$150
Roulette ($5 plus, $25 spread)	$5,000
Texas Hold'Em live poker (4-8-8)	$200
Texas Hold'Em live poker (2-4)	$100
Texas Hold'Em live poker (3-6)	$300
Texas Hold'Em live poker (5-10)	$400
Texas Hold'Em live poker (10-20)	$500
Texas Hold'Em live poker (20-40+)	$1,000
Seven-Card Stud live poker (1-4)	$150
Seven-Card Stud live poker (1-5)	$200
Seven-Card Stud live poker (1-10)	$300
Seven-Card Stud live poker (5-10)	$300
Seven-Card Stud live poker (10-20)	$500
Seven-Card Stud live poker (20-40+)	$1,000
Progressive Caribbean Stud ($5 ante)	$600
Double Down Stud ($5 table)	$200
Pai Gow Poker ($25 table)	$1,000
Pai Gow Poker ($10 table)	$500
Caribbean Draw ($5 table)	$150
Super Nines ($5 table)	$200
Let It Ride ($5 table)	$300
Casino War ($5 table)	$100

These general suggestions are based on the stated parameters. Some may differ from those I have previously listed for these games. In this book I am concentrating more on the mathematically sound principles of playing, and on the "costs" of the games based on their generally higher house edge. Also, many of these games have varying pay tables, and even much more varying bonus pay structures. Some games have vigs; others may have surrender options or other side bet features. Therefore, it is difficult to quantify each bankroll requirement to each specific game, particularly because each such decision is so highly dependent on individual circumstances, and your ability to play these games as well as they can be played.

These *guidelines* are designed to be a framework around which you can build your own bankroll. Using these examples will help you develop your own budget, based on the circumstances only you know. I have no way of knowing exactly how aggressive you may be in your gaming. Perhaps you may have a larger bankroll than others and decide to go for really aggressive plays. You per-game expenditure could easily be $1,000 per hand, or even more. Therefore, you will require a very much larger bankroll. For others, perhaps the approach is in the vastly more moderate category. How do you judge? The only sure way to find out is to analyze your own financial situation, your own abilities and dedication to the game, and your goals. Put all of that together with the other Keys to Winning, and the rest of the information and knowledge in this book, and you will be well on your way toward making the best decision possible for you.

Just to make certain that I make this point quite clear, I can assure you that you can play most of these games very enjoyably for a total $300 bankroll, divided into three sessions of about $100 each. Playing some of these games this way should assure you of about four hours of fun. Again, it's all highly relative to you, and your goals, expectations, and ability to sustain losses while awaiting the wins, and how much you are able to allocate to your bankroll. These factors, combined with all of the others shown here, ultimately determine where you can reasonably expect to be in your bankroll decisions and resultant game value decisions.

SELECTION

This is the part where "skill" in your play comes into the picture. Many people believe that when playing these games, winning is purely dependent on luck. It is correct that most of these games are passive games and, therefore, you cannot control the outcome of the events; however, it is not correct to say that playing these games involves no skills. I don't mean merely the skills of being able to play. I am referring to skills such as game selection, hand selection, how many sessions, size of the wager selection, playing progressives or not, playing conservatively or aggressively, payoff tables, play methodology selection, size of bankroll, play duration, time *when* to play, *which* casinos to play, and the remaining variety of various applied skills you will acquire as you put your own abilities into practice. There is a lot more to being a winning player than just to show up in the casino and put your money on the table.

Each of these skills is part of the "learning curve," and "comfort zone," which all of us have to reach. By acquiring these skills, you can become not only more knowledgeable, but also more comfortable. You will find that you are no longer a victim to the mere chance of luckily selecting just the right events at the right time, but that you actually will be able to select the best game with the right combinations and ways for the right reasons. You will now be able to approach your casino visit with the ability to look specifically for the kinds of situations you know are among the better options, and do so with a solid plan of attack. Not only will this result in more confidence and comfort for you when you play, but it will directly translate to regular profits. Although you won't win every time, or perhaps achieve your win goal every time you play, you will now be able to realize that this is a part of the overall approach to the game. You will no longer be a victim of emotional swings, such as deep disappointment when you don't win or reckless exuberance when you do. Although curbing these emotional reactions is part of patience, discussed above, and also discipline, discussed below, these selection skills will contribute to your overall Keys to Winning in a way in which the game and its options and complexities will no longer keep the "secret," but will divulge it to you, because you now know what to look for and how to do it to your best advantage.

DISCIPLINE

Of all the Keys to Winning, this one sounds the simplest, but it is the hardest of them all. Most of us understand the value of discipline, especially when it comes to our money. This is accentuated when we talk about the casino environment. Everything in the casino is designed to separate us from any sense of reality. The casinos are a wondrous land, where everything seems possible, as long as you still have money. Money is the lifeblood of all of this excitement. Without it, you are nothing more than dead wood, and you will be flushed out in a hurry. Having discipline as part of your winning objectives saves you from the inglorious fate of being washed clean, hung out to dry, and tossed away as yet another victim of the ill-prepared and unwary. Having discipline as part of your tricks of the trade when you go gambling simply means to make the commitment to play wisely, with reason, with goals in mind. In fact, playing with all of the empowering Keys to Winning, as well as all the other information I have shared here. If you want to have your "mad time," that's okay too. Budget for it, realize it, recognize it, place it as part of your overall game plan. Even that can become part of your discipline, as long as you don't let the thrill overwhelm you or allow it to completely drown all your plans and your discipline along with it.

Unfortunately, *making* a commitment to self-discipline when going to the casino, is very easy. *Keeping to it* once you get to the casino is very hard. So hard, in fact, that most individuals who arrive at the casino completely convinced they will not allow this experience to get the better of them do just that. And fast, often as soon as they walk through the door. Suddenly, they see the excitement, the games, the flashing lights, the sounds of money and chips—the entire atmosphere captures them. In the door they go, and out the door go all of their well-meaning and carefully conceived plans. Also their sense of discipline. It happens to just about everyone, even hardened veterans of the casino lifestyle. All of us are human beings, and we are not perfect. We have failures, and the lack of discipline is the greatest failure of all. Most people who go to casinos don't understand what "discipline" really is or how it applies to their gaming success or financial failure.

To offer the easiest guideline, discipline in gambling simply means to remain conscious of the value of your money, and conscious of your desired goals and objectives. It means, mostly, to not allow yourself to be drawn into the very comfortable, but very financially deadly, sense of "why not, it's only money" syndrome. Once you have experienced the casino lifestyle a few times, you will often hear many people say things like that. These people are trapped in the losses they have incurred and are now trying to rationalize it for themselves. They don't expect anyone else to be listening to them, or to really understand what expressions such as this really mean. They have resigned themselves to the loss of all their money, and to the "I no longer care" attitude. That's the danger sign. Once you stop caring about the value of the money you are using to play—or are winning— then you have lost the discipline that comes with realizing that this money isn't just coins, tokens, or gaming chips. This money actually spends, the way it does when buying food or gas for your car, when paying bills, and so on. It is real money, and it has real meaning. Discipline means to *remember* this, and play accordingly.

This doesn't mean that you must be, or should be, a miser. Playing too carefully is also a prescription for disaster. I have already mentioned that "scared" money flies away quickly. Don't play that way. To win, you must play aggressively and with a sufficient bankroll to justify your level of action. All of this is covered in the other Keys to Winning. Discipline is the glue that holds it all together. Once the glue stops holding, it all falls apart.

WIN GOALS

What is a win goal? In simplest terms, a win goal is the realistic expectation of a certain win amount, based on the potential of available wins relative to the bankroll allowed, session stake allocated, expertise at the game, plus time at the game. This simple formula will equal your end-result profitability, in winning situations, and end-result saving of money that would have been lost in negative situations.

For example, most gamblers will say that a 2 percent win goal over and above the session stake is a very great achievement. The casino, for example, has a win goal of around 2 percent for most blackjack games, and an average of about 20 percent over all the table games they offer. Some games will make them even more money because people will play them badly. Although basic blackjack, for example, can be played to less than 0.5 percent casino advantage, most players will play the game so badly that the casinos actually yield anywhere from 2 percent to 6 percent, and often even more, on a game which can actually yield a *player* advantage if played properly and with skill (for more information on blackjack, I refer you to my book: *Powerful Profits from Blackjack*).

For many of the games in this book, the average expectation is from around 15 percent to perhaps 28 percent, depending on the casino, where it is located, and what the competition is like. In Las Vegas, the casinos mostly count on around 15 percent as their *average* win goal for all of these games. The difference between the casino and the player is that the casino can easily have a much lower win goal, because their doors are open "24/7/365." Their games make money all the time—every hour, every day, every week, every month, every year—without ever needing a rest or a break. We can't play like that. While the casino can easily offer a game that can reasonably expect to yield less than 1 percent profit, it will get this all the time, always, over the short term as well as the long haul. You, the player, can't play like that. Gamblers in general must have win goals not only commensurate with their bankroll, session stakes, and so on, as listed earlier, but also with the realization that their exposure to the game will only be a very short slice of the game's overall event reality. Therefore, such win goals cannot—and should not—be measured in percentages relative to the way the casinos figure their own odds and win goals. Rather, your win goals should be measured in terms of what the game *can yield,* especially if played correctly, and if selected in accordance with the various selection criteria I listed earlier. It is also important at this point to introduce a derivative of the win goal criterion, called the win expectation.

The win goal is what you have set as your desired objective, realistically based on the various principles already demonstrated. The win *expectation,* however, is based within the reality of the game itself and, most specifically, in that very short-term slice of that one specific game's event experience. The point is that throughout your casino visit, no playing session is ever independent of your other sessions. All your playing sessions are combined to reveal, in the end as you go home, the entire block of *all* sessions. Whatever results you have achieved at that point determine your average per session win expectation percentage, and your win goal achievement levels. You can use this information to reflect on how well you played, and to modify your goals and expectations for future visits. But you must take *everything* into account, even the value of all the additions you have earned, such as comps and freebies, and club points. All of this combines to affect your goals, expectations, and final relative results.

This now brings us to the final item in this chapter, and that is the overall win goals and overall win expectation. This is set by you, based on bankroll, skill, and other abilities, as well as whatever other information and skills you may have acquired. If you have understood what I have attempted to illustrate, your total win goal for your casino visit should be directly relative to your bankroll, your comfort level at the games, and your gaming and playing skills, including selection skills.

As a guide, your overall win *goal* should be to double your bankroll. Your win *expectation* should be to come home with 20 percent over and above your bring-in bankroll. If you achieve anything close to this, you have beaten the casino. You have done what *less than 1 percent of all casino players are able to do.* You have become a good, knowledgeable, and responsible player.

Congratulations!

Postscript

This book is a potpourri of casino table games. There are many of these games in every casino, but most of them are either not very complex, or not so popular as to warrant a whole book just about them. That's why I have put them all together and created this book in the way it was done. This is the ninth book in my *Powerful Profits* series from Kensington Books. Owning all of these books will give you twenty years of knowledge and experience that I have lived, and put into these books. While there are many other books about these various casino games, the books I have created speak from the direct experience of a player and casino consultant. I have been on both sides of the games—as a gambler and as a casino employee. My job as a casino consultant was to write reports about various items pertaining to casino operations and how the players perceived the casino. This I was able to do after many years as a player. I knew how the players felt and what they wanted. I also knew how the casinos operated, and what *they* wanted. In my books, I tell you the truth about these games in the *real world,* in the real casinos, and as you will find them when you go there.

Although I enjoy the theory of gaming, let me tell you that some 99 percent of all casino players of these games will never be able to play those games purely and only in accordance with the theory, or with the mathematically perfect strategies. It simply isn't possible to do so. Not only have the casinos changed, and the games changed, but the casinos aren't stupid—they have experts who are better at these "systems" than the people who are trying to play them. Even if you can still find a casino that will allow you to play blackjack with all of the best mathematically advantageous rules, for example, and still allow you to count cards, just precisely how well can you do it? For how long? Not well, and not for long, and that's just the plain, simple truth. Even a casino that will give you a perfect blackjack game that's juicily great for a card counter—even if that were still possible—such casinos would limit your spread to no more than four units, and probably cap your bets at $25 a hand. So, what good is that to you? How much will you make? Not much. This doesn't mean that blackjack isn't a good game to play, or that you can't win playing it. In my books *Powerful Profits from Blackjack,* and *Powerful Profits: Winning Strategies for Casino Games,* I show you how even a casual player can make blackjack into a good game, and make profits even in the short term, without the need for the complex card counting systems. In fact, I call all my strategies "methods," because they are just that—methods developed over decades of research, trial, error, and actual in-casino real-world play.

My opinions about casino games aren't limited to only blackjack. I have opinions about every casino game, and in my series I have taken several years of my life to outline precisely what these opinions are, and why I have them. They are all designed to let you in on the biggest secret of gambling:

Just because the theory of the game says that something should happen X percent of the time, this doesn't mean that it will, and it doesn't mean that it will do so at precisely that small instance of your play at that game.

Therefore, while knowing the theory behind each game is important, as is the total knowledge of what all these games are, and although knowing all the percentages is equally and profoundly important, the reality is that basing your life's gambling on these theories will inevitably lead to disappointment and eventual loss of your money. The real world doesn't revolve around the statistics. The statistics merely *reflect* what we—as human beings—*assume the reality of these events to be.* And just because we say so doesn't mean that that's what it is. It simply means that those among us who have developed knowledge in numbers, odds, and percentages have reached a general consensus that such events, as identified, will be given that X percent value, and that therefore everyone will so understand them and deal with those events accordingly. This is a wonderful experience and a terrific exercise in logic and mathematics. Although useful as a guideline in the real world of the real casino, such thinking doesn't do a whole lot for your wish to win money at this precise game in this precise moment, this day, this hour, this trip to the casino. On average, a person would most likely have to play about fifty-five years in order to come anywhere near close to what the generalized statistics indicate of the mathematical frequencies of occurrence for stated events. It really doesn't do a whole lot for anyone planning a vacation to a casino today.

There are a few players, however, who are true gambling professionals. They are the small minority of true gamblers, of which there are fewer and fewer each year as casinos learn to combat them and their skills. Surveillance technologies are now able to identify a person from the picture the cameras take as he is walking into the casino, and other tracking technology such as in-chip transmitters that instantly identify the chip and denomination being wagered. These devices make true professional gambling just about a thing of the past. Most of the professional gamblers who are around these days are poker players, and most of the big-money players play on the poker tournament circuit. There are others who still play in the private games, and some that play in ring games, but as the casinos get more sophisticated in learning the various ways in which gamblers win consistently—those gamblers who do this legally, of course—the availability of games good enough for a professional casino gambler to make a living from is becoming very sparse. As a result, the traditional casino shark is now all but extinct.

Such professional casino gamblers play every day, and for many hours. Primarily for this reason, they are players who must play closest to the theory of the game. The event frequencies of their exposure to the games are very much higher than those of the casual player, even if such a casual player is a regular casino visitor and may even play as often as every day. What separates a "professional" from a "regular" is the object of the visit: the "regular" goes there because that's what she has chosen as her recreation. The true casino professional, on the other hand, goes to the casino with only one objective, and that's to make money. Such a professional player will have a specific financial goal for the day, and once reached, he leaves because he knows he has another session later, or the next day, and he also knows that the longer he stays in the game, the greater the likelihood of the eventual theoretical mathematics to erode his hard-gotten wins. It is for this less than 1 percent of casino players that the theory of the game and the application of the mathematically derived strategies are most useful, and crucial to success. Of course, any such professional will also quickly tell you that knowing the math and being able to win money are not necessarily the same thing. Sometimes you must throw away the math and go with the flow—translation: Sometimes you have to play with the *reality* of what's happening rather than with the theory as mathematically quantified. What does this mean? Well, dear friend, this means exactly what I have been telling you all along: To win money playing casino games you must not only have the knowledge of the game, and the knowledge of the game's math, odds, and percentages, but also be able to step away from it and play to win in accordance with the reality of what is actually happening. That's what separates the regular winners from those who merely get lucky sometimes.

In the movie and song *The Gambler*, singer and actor Kenny Rogers puts it simply, but to the point: "You've got to know when to hold 'em, know when to fold 'em." This applies to all casino games—you've got to know the game, and its details, including the math, odds, and percentages, but you also must have the ability to step away from that theory and go with the application of the practical strategy for winning in the short term. This means to "know when to hold 'em" and "when to fold 'em." Although quite quaint as an explanation, this is the real truth of casino gambling—know the game, know the theory, but know when to step away from it and why. That's how you will make powerful profits from casino games.

I now wish you good luck, good fortune, and thank you for the time we shared together discussing casino games.

Acknowledgments

Many people have contributed in some way to this book, and have influenced my life. I dedicate this book to my dear mother, because her life has been of such profound meaning, and of such complexity, that her story is a book in itself. It is an everlasting credit to her that she has not only retained her life and her sanity, but that she is still able to contribute to and foster our family. She is by far the most deserving person to whom I ever can so offer my thanks.

I also wish to thank my literary agents, Greg Dinkin and Frank Scatoni. Through their agency, Venture Literary, they recognized the value of what I had to offer as an author of books on casino games and gaming. Without their efforts, this book, and the others in this series, would never have come to exist.

My thanks also to Bruce Bender, a managing director at Kensington Publishing. He recognized that this book, and this series, offers valuable insight into the casino games as they really are, and will enable almost all players to realize a happy and profitable casino experience. I thank Bruce, and the staff at Kensington, for their help in this process. In particular, I wish to single out a lady who has become my friend, my editor, the lovely Ann LaFarge.

I also wish to thank my colleagues and staff at the *Midwest Gaming and Travel* magazine, particularly Cathy Jaeger and Beth. I have known Cathy for a long time, and she was at one time also the editor of several other magazines that published my articles. Since 1984 I have published a continuous column on casino gaming in various publications, and for most of these years it was Cathy who was my editor and friend.

In addition, I wish to single out Michael Shackleford, better known to all as "the Wizard of Odds." Michael is a terrific mathematician and analyst of casino games. His website, www.wizardofodds.com, is full of wonderful information about casino games and their odds. I have used Michael's website as a reference source, and to complement and verify my own calculations as I have needed them. I have found his work of great help, especially when I tried to separate the theory from the reality. I wish to thank him for the work that he has done, and for the invaluable assistance it offers to players of casino games. I also wish to encourage anyone with interest in casino games and game analysis to contact Michael and request his consulting services. Only my late colleague Lenny Frome was as brilliant a mathematician and gambling game analyst as is Michael. Michael has great skills that allow the world of mathematics to become more clearly visible to the casual player, and although I do not always see eye to eye with theoretical mathematics, I nonetheless have a deep appreciation for the skill it takes to be able to do what Michael does so well.

I am fortunate to also bring you a list of my friends and others who have helped me and influenced my life in many ways.

I extend my gratitude and thanks to my longtime friend Tom Caldwell for the many things he has done to help me and to enrich my life. I have had many discussions with Tom, and my thoughts about the casino games have become more mature because of these discussions. I also send my thanks to Norreta, Sean, and Brent, for reasons they all know.

To the management and staff of Arizona Charlie's Hotel and Casino, in Las Vegas, in particular those in the poker room, and to all my other friends and associates in the gaming business, from owners, managers, senior executives, hosts, and supervisors, you all know who you are, and I thank you.

My friends in Australia, Neil and his family, Lilli and little MRM (Mark), Ormond College, University of Melbourne, the governor of Victoria and my former master, Sir Davis McCaughey. Also his Proctorial Eminence R.A. Dwyer, Esq., and the Alumni Association of the University of Wollongong, NSW, Department of Philosophy, and Professor Chipman.

My thanks also to the management and staff of the newspaper *The Age,* in Melbourne, Australia, where I once worked, and also to the *Fairfax Press,* Sydney, Australia, and the management and staff of the *Ilawarra Mercury* newspaper, in Wollongong, NSW, Australia.

I also extend my grateful appreciation to Laurence E. Levit, C.P.A. of Los Angeles, who has been my steadfast friend, accountant, and adviser for two decades, and whose faith in me and my work has never faltered. A truer friend a man rarely finds. And also to Michael Harrison, attorney at law in Beverly Hills, California, whose expertise and help have always made my life more secure.

To Andrew Hooker and the "Cowboys" from Vietnam, I also send my thanks. And to Edwin Slogar, a good friend.

And finally to all those whose paths have crossed with mine, and who have for one reason or another stopped a while and visited. I may no longer remember your names, by I do remember what it meant to have those moments. Thank you.

Index